FEMINISTS DON'T WEAR **PINK**
and other lies

AMAZING WOMEN ON WHAT
THE F-WORD MEANS TO THEM

CURATED BY

scarlett curtis

PENGUIN BOOKS

PENGUIN BOOKS

UK | USA | Canada | Ireland | Australia
India | New Zealand | South Africa

Penguin Books is part of the Penguin Random House group of companies
whose addresses can be found at global.penguinrandomhouse.com.

www.penguin.co.uk   www.puffin.co.uk   www.ladybird.co.uk

First published 2018
This edition published 2020

005

Text design by Mandy Norman
Cover design by Cat Lobo
Set in Sabon LT Pro 10pt/17pt
Printed and bound in Great Britain by Clays Ltd, Elcograf S.p.A.

A CIP catalogue record for this book is available from the British Library

ISBN: 978-0-241-41836-9

All correspondence to:
Penguin Books, Penguin Random House Children's
80 Strand, London WC2R 0RL

FEMINISTS DON'T WEAR PINK

and other lies

Contents

ANGER

JOY 177

POETRY BREAK 213

ACTION 237

FOREWORD

BY

Girl Up

At Girl Up, feminism is one of our favourite words – and it's different, and awesome, wherever you go. Just as every girl around the world has her own unique story to tell, she also has her own particular version of what feminism means to her. No two people experience feminism in the same way, but each perspective is valid and important. Girl Up is a global leadership development initiative, positioning girls to be leaders in the movement for gender equality. We're building a community that is working towards a world where every girl has an equal opportunity to reach her full potential and change the world, regardless of race, religion, ethnicity, sexual orientation, age or ability. Every girl has a unique and powerful story to tell. We celebrate these stories and the diversity of our movement across our global community.

WHERE WE ARE

Girl Up has more than 2,200 clubs in over a hundred countries, and we've trained 40,000 girls from all backgrounds to create tangible change for girls everywhere. Girl Up has empowered young women leaders to defend gender equality and equal rights for every girl.

WHAT WE DO

Girl Up provides leadership training and gives girls the tools to become gender-equality advocates and activists. Through our programmes, girls broaden their social-impact skill set, receive a platform to tell their stories and apply STEM* for social good. Our girl leaders create real policy change at local and national levels, and raise millions of dollars to support United Nations programmes that reach tens of thousands of girls around the world and to build community-based movements. Girl Up is an initiative of the UN Foundation, working across a global community of partners to achieve gender equality worldwide.

WANT TO JOIN US?

Our movement is reaching every corner of the globe and we want YOU to be a part of it. If you're at secondary school or university, girl or boy, you can join Girl Up and start taking action for gender equality today. But it's not just students who can join! You can run a race with Team Girl Up, join a Girl Up Young Professionals meetup, or connect us with your organization to partner with Girl Up.

Learn more at GirlUp.org/Join.

* Science, Technology, Engineering and Mathematics

"EVERY GIRL HAS A UNIQUE AND POWERFUL STORY TO TELL. WE CELEBRATE THESE STORIES AND THE DIVERSITY OF OUR MOVEMENT ACROSS OUR GLOBAL COMMUNITY.**"**

INTRODUCTION

BY

Scarlett Curtis

JOURNALIST, ACTIVIST

I didn't know I was a feminist until I was fifteen. I didn't know I was a feminist because I didn't know I needed to be, and I also didn't think I would still be allowed to wear make-up if I became one. And I seriously loved make-up. I went to school just like my brothers, my mum had a job just like my dad. Feminism was something that we learned about in history class and didn't have to worry about any more. Like telegrams or corsets or the plague, feminism was the stuff of suffragettes and burnt bras and fights that had been won and long forgotten.

Much like a rare breed of bird, I knew feminists still existed out there in the wild. I also knew I most definitely did not want to be one. For starters, it was the middle of the noughties, and in a world where Beyoncé existed I couldn't fathom what on earth these feminists were fighting for. More importantly my image of a 'feminist' was entirely in opposition to every single priority my fifteen-year-old brain possessed. Feminists didn't use make-up (my favourite hobby). They didn't shave their legs (my favourite form of exercise). Feminists didn't like boys (my favourite type of human) and, most importantly, feminists definitely didn't wear pink. And pink was my favourite colour. Being a feminist would mean disposing of half my wardrobe, revealing my spotty skin and hairy legs to the world and putting an end to the twenty-plus daily MSN messages I sent to boys I had crushes on.

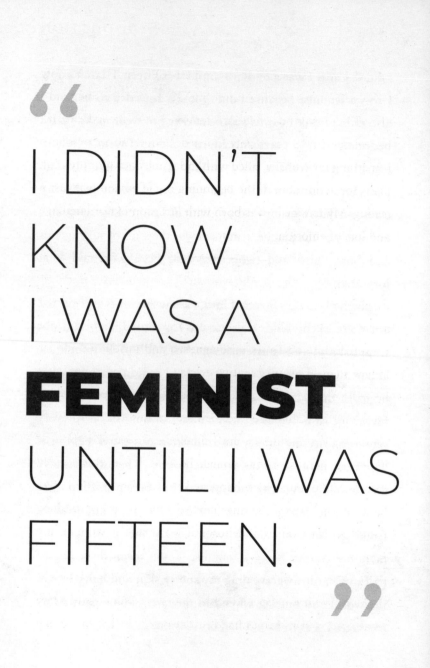

" I DIDN'T KNOW I WAS A **FEMINIST** UNTIL I WAS FIFTEEN. "

There's an amazing feminist superhero called Audre Lorde who said: 'Our feelings are our most genuine paths to knowledge.' My nosedive into feminism was fuelled entirely by feelings. In the years since, it has developed and grown into something far wordier, filled with thoughts, books, quotes and plans for action; but at the beginning my feminism was just a feeling. My feminism was born with little context or language and lots of emotion.

When I was fifteen I was treated very badly by a group of men and a few women who wouldn't have treated me that way if I had been a man. I was a teenage girl with blue dip-dyed hair and a predilection for wearing tutus to hospital appointments. I was very ill and I was misdiagnosed and mistreated for far longer than even an irritating teenager who could probably have done with being knocked down a few pegs deserves to be. I was mistreated and silenced for a number of reasons that only now, nearly a decade on, am I finally beginning to unpick. It happened because I was young, because I was emotionally 'complicated', but it also happened because I was a girl. And because the person sitting next to me in every waiting room, doctor's office and hospital ward was a woman and a mother.

In the grand scheme of heinous acts committed by the patriarchy, what happened to me was very small. It was very small and it got better, and I'm extremely lucky. But it did happen. And it sparked a feeling inside me; and that feeling began to grow.

My illness also meant that I spent three years of my life lying in my bedroom with nothing much to do except read and Google and knit small animals. So I began to read. I read Virginia Woolf and Gloria Steinem and Caitlin Moran and then realized they were all white women and I might need to start looking a little further. I read Audre Lorde and Roxane Gay and Chimamanda Ngozi Adichie, and slowly but surely I began to understand and think and see.

I began to understand that what had happened to me was a small ripple that took place in an ocean of pain, movement and change. I began to understand that gender equality was not in fact a thing of the past but a far-off dream for the future. A dream that generations of women and men had been fighting for and continued to fight for every single day.

Once I began to understand that, I also began to understand that the assumptions I had held about what it meant to be a feminist were in fact a tool of the very systems of hate that these women were trying to smash. This system of hate (also known as 'the patriarchy') had concocted an image of a feminist precisely so young women would be deterred from continuing the fight. The lies we have been told about feminism have been fed to us to hold us back from a movement that is actually for everyone. A movement that is more beautiful and more potentially powerful than we could ever have dreamed. As I began to read I began to understand that feminists do in fact wear make-up (if they want to). They also shave their legs (if they want to) and love boys (if they want to). Feminists can also definitely wear pink, a lot of pink.

The women's movement has been alive and kicking for a very long time now. It is a beautiful and complicated timeline of people, theories, words and books that are constantly defining and redefining what it means to be a feminist. This book is not an academic textbook. It is not a manual on how to be a perfect feminist or a book of essays by professors of women's studies explaining the history of the movement. Those books exist, and many of them are brilliant, but that is not what this book is.

This book is a book of feelings that are transforming into thoughts that are transforming into action. Most of the amazing women who have contributed to this book probably don't know much more about feminism than you do. Most of the women are just at the starting line of the lifelong journey to discover what it means to be a feminist and to fight the feminist fight. This book is not here to tell you everything you need to know about feminism, it's here to show you that at the heart of feminism is women. Women who are complex and complicated, who wear make-up and wear pink and laugh and cry and get confused just like you. This book is here to hopefully show you that being a feminist isn't quite what you thought it was.

While my fifteen-year-old self was wrong about a lot of things, she was right about one thing. Feminists are rare birds. They are rare birds who fly above us, trying to look down and see the world for what it is. They look down and see the mountains that our world will have to overcome if freedom is ever going to be possible, and then they fly back down to earth to help us all with the climb. I am a feminist. And boy do I wear pink.

" THIS BOOK
IS HERE TO
SHOW YOU
THAT AT THE
HEART OF
FEMINISM IS
WOMEN.
"

THE FIVE STAGES
OF FEMINISM

BY

Scarlett Curtis

JOURNALIST, ACTIVIST

Becoming a feminist isn't something that happens to a woman overnight. No one on this planet was born understanding the complicated, overlapping and often confusing elements that this mighty word holds within it. Unfortunately, there's also no magic feminist fairy that flies around gifting people the power of rational argument, a grasp of intersectional politics and an ability to organize activism. A person's journey into 'feminism' is a constant state of learning, re-learning, feeling and understanding. I understand more about how to be a true feminist today than I did yesterday, and less than I will tomorrow, and I hope to continue like this for the rest of my life.

While no two people's paths into feminism are the same, we've broken up the wonderful personal stories in this book into the five stages of feminism. They take you from EPIPHANY all the way to ACTION and EDUCATION, and we hope they might help you to navigate this bumpy road into your own feminist awakening.

These stages of feminism are open to anyone willing to embrace them – a well-trodden path that thousands of men and women choose to embark upon each year. Let this book be your guide, and let it also provide a little bit of comfort in the knowledge that whatever you feel, be it anger, confusion, joy or solidarity, it's all OK, it will all be OK, we will make it OK.

EPIPHANY

noun; *pronunciation* ɪˈpɪf.ᵊn.i

a moment when you suddenly feel that you understand, or suddenly become conscious of, something that is very important to you

Oprah would call this your Aha! moment, and many feminists in fact find that their own Aha! feminist moments coincide with a deepening of their love for Oprah!

MY FEMINISM

BY

Saoirse Ronan

ACTOR

Feminism did not happen to me. Feminism was not one moment. Instead it has been the result of a series of events throughout my life, and the people who turned each of those events into a tiny informative experience. For example, when I was lucky enough to meet my activist best friend at twenty-one, who pretty rapidly made me realize that feminism and what it means to be a feminist was right there inside me all along – deeply understood and ready to make itself known!

MY FEMINISM

MOTHERS:
Watching and learning.
Questions. Hugs.
Period talk. Boy/girl talk.
Random sing-alongs in the car in the rain. Pushing away.
Returning again and again.

HOME:
Belonging to it.
Leaving it. Finding your own way back to it.
Picking up your people along the winding way.

HELP:

Accepting it.

Listening out for it.

Giving it back.

WORK:

Caring about it.

Fighting for it.

Living for it.

Living without it.

Putting heads together to create it.

Knowing what you want.

DISCOVERING:

Music. Films. Books. *Bridesmaids* (the movie). Love. People.
Sex. Your body – 'What the hell is that?! Is that normal?
Does that happen to you too? Oh, it does?! OK. PHEW!
Thought I was the only one.'

BEING:

On your own.

In a group.

Scared shitless.

Confident.

Honest with yourself as much as possible.

GIRLS:

Loving them.

Working with them.

Cheering them on.

Playing football with them.

Laughing and dancing with them.

Asking them about their parents.

BOYS:

Loving them.

Working with them.

Cheering them on.

Playing football with them.

Laughing and dancing with them.

Asking them about their parents.

Feminism, for me, is the quiet kid in the corner of the classroom who doesn't talk much. The kid you don't even notice is there, until one day you're performing in the annual school show and she takes centre stage, only to belt out a Whitney ballad like nobody's business. Boy, do you take notice of her then. You will never not take notice again.

CAT WOMEN

BY

Evanna Lynch

ACTOR

I'm sitting in the office of a well-respected casting director in New York, making amiable conversation and desperately trying not to bleed through to this woman's couch. The meeting had swiftly taken a turn for the better when I reached for my conversational jackpot piece and struck gold – the casting director was also a cat lady.

Her eyes light up as I mention how I flew my beloved sidekick, a precious Persian by the name of Puff, across the ocean to room with me for two months in New York City. It's a risky move, mentioning a cat in this environment, when statistically, a career woman living in New York is much more likely to have a dog (office-trained, travels well, the size of a small bag of groceries) and if she does, she will swiftly judge me and end the meeting sooner than anticipated, or worse, she will feel my own irrepressible disdain for dog people and I'll never hear from her again. But, oh joy, she has a cat! Two cats, in fact!

Suddenly, we are gal-pals. Suddenly, I feel rays of light emanating from my career prospects, which have just brightened considerably. We will make movies together, Mrs Reputable New-York-City Casting Lady and I! She will think of me when casting her next quirky independent rom-com and I'll audition, winningly, and afterwards she'll ask, 'How is your sweet, sweet cat?' and I'll say, 'Great, thank you, hope one day you'll get to meet her,' and she'll wink and call my agent the minute I leave the room – because cat ladies look out for each other.

This delightful series of events and beyond whizzes through my mind as I lean forward, phone outstretched, to share with her the outtakes of the latest most adorable series of photos of Puff lounging in a strip of sunlight, when I feel it: that curious, not uncomfortable, stomach-flipping sensation – whether with joy or horror, it is entirely situational – of uterine lining unmistakably falling from somewhere within your lower midriff to somewhere you hope and pray, in that moment of prolonged suspension, is generously, gloriously padded.

You may unclench your Kegels, however, dear reader, and rest assured that I was wearing those moisture-wicking, period-drinking, feminist wonder-panties that Facebook bullies people into buying. Unfortunately for me, I'd chosen the day of an important meeting to test-drive these much-hyped panties and I should mention, dear horrified male reader, that when you've been plugging your most vexatious orifice sealed snug with super-plus tampons for the last ten years of menstrual activity, the distinctive *drop* feeling can be extremely jarring and frankly panic-attack inducing.

I don't know what possessed me to buy them, the panties. I'm not good with bodily functions; I ghosted and eventually unfriended a girl who potentially heard me fart through a thin bathroom wall (I hope you're well, Vicky); I cover my ears and wail in distress when my American girlfriends exchange 'poop' stories; I can forgive just about any bad behaviour from boyfriends – mysterious disappearances, tardiness, prefers men – so long as he smells dreamy. But one evening, while browsing Facebook, there were the panties, again, in my face. There was Mila Kunis, eyes wide, inhibitions vanished, eulogizing the period panties in a short promotional video. And even though I didn't have a particularly strong affinity with Mila Kunis, and even though I hated the idea of my menstrual blood pooling in my knickers and staying there defiantly, and even though I've only ever felt cascading waves of gratitude for the invention of the tampon, that evening, I felt I ought to have the panties. I liked the super-sassy vibes Mila was giving and she seemed so suitably, impressively feminist, in the not-nuanced, very blatant sense of the word, unashamedly discussing the particulars of her menstrual cycle with Facebook.

I'd been reading feminist books and learning that our bodies are the four seasons, and the patriarchy structured the working week with only the male reproductive system in mind, and I was feeling kinda guilty that I didn't have a #MeToo status up and it just seemed like the right, progressive, *feminist* thing to do and yes, I was actually kind of excited to be an empowered bleeding woman, dancing in circles in the streets in my new feminist knickers. So I added three pairs to my cart, clicked COMPLETE ORDER and vowed to be a better advocate for women.

And yet, as I sat there, seeping my way into an uncharted likely public humiliation on the oblivious casting director's couch and flicking through her cat pictures with insulting rapidity, all I could really think was *Fuck Feminism!*

I am confused by feminism, needless to say. It's been a generally confusing time for me, seeing many women I admire speak up about their experiences of oppression at the hands of men, and feeling like an alien who dropped in from a much nicer planet.

'Am I a feminist?' I wonder, for perhaps the first time in my twenty-six-plus years as a woman, because I've never really entertained the thought that I'm not. *Obviously!* my mind counters quickly, but there is an annoying, niggling thought that I need to be doing more to show it.

So I take it up with the woman who knows me best, but who I can't recall ever instilled in me the importance of asserting feminist values, other than facilitating myself and my sisters to be whatever kind of women we'd like to be.

'Am I a feminist, Mum?' I ask her bluntly. She's as thrown

by the question as I was, wondering aloud why ever would you not be.

Do you believe in equal rights for men and women?

Do you believe women should work?

Do you believe men and women are of equal intellectual capability?

Yes! Yes, I tell her, and, well, actually I would wager that on average women surpass men in intelligence, but that is a mere opinion.

'Then you're a feminist,' she affirms, before adding, 'Sure, just remember how taken you were with the Disney princesses when you were younger! They were your feminist icons, I'd say.' My heart sinks, hearing that last bit, knowing it to be true and that I'll always have to lie in conversation about feminism and my original heroines. Or maybe it is my mind that sinks, recalling the feminist think pieces that declared Belle a delusional, powerless victim of Stockholm Syndrome, and Ariel a bad influence on young girls for cleaving herself in two in exchange for legs, and yes, a vagina that a prince could love.

My heart, on the other hand, soars at the mention of the dynamic princesses of fairy-tale dreams, their lofty ideas, hopeful hearts and glorious tresses. I agree with my mum, shrug off the notion of feminism for tonight and rewatch *The Swan Princess* for the second time this month. Tomorrow, I decide,

I'll dredge up Matilda, Jo March and Hermione Granger who I can cite as suitably studious, substantial literary feminist influences, all of whom I liked but didn't idolize, unfortunately. No, I can't tell the truth, I tell myself as I watch Odette transform from a graceful swan to an even more enchanting lady form, all waves and curves and delicate limbs.

She is just too feminine to be a feminist.

I'm not sure when I first began to define what a woman could be, and could not be, but all of my teenage years are permeated with the memory of the belief that books were for me and beauty was for others. Somewhere along the way I latched on to the idea that women of substance, politically conscious, world-changing women worth paying attention to, were above the frivolities of feminine indulgences. Reading *Vogue* and *Elle* I learned that beauty was painfully exclusive, that cheekbones and skinny genes and wealth were the assets you needed, and I began to see prettiness as a foreign world I had no place in. I grew to resent feminine women and decided that a woman simply could not be charming and clever at once; you had to pick one and I knew which one garnered respect, if not desire. I'd dress in clashing prints, spangly bug earrings and bold tights because quirky girls *had thoughts*, *were interesting*, and those girls sashaying around town in crop tops with belly-button piercings blinking ostentatiously most definitely had no thoughts to spare for anything outside the sphere of their own physical perfection.

I'd stroll past my crush, nose buried in *Anna Karenina*, wondering agonizingly when he'd notice my depth, substance and most commendable abstention from low-cut tops and desperate bids to be an object of sexual fascination. And there was even that time I dressed as Harry Potter for the school graduation party as a silent, ironic protest against the fishnet stockings and streakily applied tans of my less censorious peers. I thought I was hilarious and mature, but when an attractive boy glanced at me across the room, with my orange juice and smudgy lightning-scar, and shook his head in disgust, I knew what he meant. But I remained confused.

I liked me, I knew me, I knew I didn't have to be beautiful to be worthy and it was much more valuable and interesting to have thoughts, dreams and plans to heal the world. It was better to spend time developing one's mind with Russian novels than with the latest reality star's diet and lifestyle coffee-table book. I'd earn respect and admiration in my career by being well-read, socially conscious and understated, whereas gluing dainty bejewelled pieces of acrylic to my nails would set me back two hours of intellectual cultivation. And yet, all the while, the expression of unbridled femininity was something I could not get over.

*

I do remember the first time a beautiful, feminine woman showed me love. I was eleven years old, bone-thin from a relentless eating disorder, standing on the steps of yet another perfect stranger my mum hoped would cure me, when she opened the door and lit up the air around her. My new therapist, all peroxide-blonde hair, shimmery skin and shunted-up bosom that refused to go unnoticed. I hunched closer into myself, feeling scared of her gaze, unworthy of her attention, feeling so hopelessly insignificant in the presence of a real-life princess.

'Hi, Beautiful!!' she bellowed out, loud enough for the whole street to hear, and she hugged me so tight I almost coughed. And then she took me in and began to help me put my broken soul and life back together. She healed me by the things she said, but mostly by who she was, a radiant, brilliant, creative, compassionate, kind, wise, sensitive, strong, soft and gorgeous woman who showed me love and consideration for an hour each week. She looked at me through those beautiful, soulful, glitter-lined eyes with love and warmth, and reflected somebody worth loving, somebody who didn't need to be punished for existing and who in fact had her own gifts to uncover.

She was the first hint that a woman could be all things. That she could mull over Osho's *Book of Secrets* while she waited for her tan to dry. Or be madly in love without losing herself. She was a wonder and a miracle and a seeming cacophony of oxymorons. She was the most powerful woman I'd ever met and for the first time I saw that feminine charm, beauty shared generously, not hidden self-consciously, was a gift and an asset, and a vehicle for change.

As I grew up and met more goddess-like women, as frivolous as they were smart and loving, I forgave myself my penchant for girly indulgences. I spent time on things that would not change the world but would make me feel good and powerful, and more capable of changing the world. And as I indulged this fascination, I felt the grip of obsession with it lessening. My knees no longer buckled at the desperately sought assertion from boys that I was 'cute'.

I know, my mind would reply drily to those shallow observations. *Next?*

But was my derision for femininity not more appropriate to express and more feminist of me? Has a patriarchal society worn me down and caused me to waste precious time and energy on pandering to the male gaze? These questions have plagued me lately as I try to find myself in the feminist conversation, to recognize someone more nuanced, more human, undeniably feminine, soft, vulnerable, and strong too. Is she so elusive? Is she just confusing people? Does femininity impede feminism?

*

A few months ago I had the chance to interview the legendary and oft controversy-stirring animal rights activist, Ingrid Newkirk, the founder and president of PETA, the largest animal rights organization in the world. I was nervous and geared myself up for a difficult conversation with this tough, undeniably fearless woman, about whom I detected no sense of vulnerability. When I picked up the Skype call, Ingrid's video flashed on and a soft-spoken blonde lady asked why we weren't going to be videoing this conversation. I explained that there's no need with a podcast and we'd never done it with video before, at which point Ingrid shared, disappointed, that she was looking 'all beautiful' and had put on make-up especially for the conversation. I laughed and relaxed as this famously outspoken and unstoppable activist bemoaned the fact that she'd taken the time to make herself up and our listeners would not get to see it.

During the interview Ingrid shared how she would still cry at night, warm in her bed, thinking of the animals who were shivering in gestation crates. And how she was temporarily distracted from founding and growing PETA into the powerful organization it is today when she got home from India and 'discovered boys'. And how she can only watch cartoons when she winds down because she witnesses so many atrocities towards animals in her daily work. In an elegant, gentle

English accent reminiscent of Princess Diana, she taught me to smile and see the best in people when explaining that fur-trim coats were made using barbaric practices, and then switched just as easily, cheerily, into explaining her posthumous plans to have her flesh barbecued in the same manner as cow flesh in order to make a point.

I sat for a few moments after the interview, stunned and happy. Here again was a woman who I thought so surely was one thing and not the other, demonstrating lightly that she could, in fact, be everything.

The perplexing thing was that after the interview was released our podcast received a handful of complaints from listeners (who mostly, it should be noted, had chosen not to listen to the interview) citing their disappointment at us for interviewing a woman who they saw as an enemy to the feminist cause. The sexualization of women in PETA's advertisements was mentioned. And a porn site that PETA launched where sexy videos were interspersed with animal rights messages.

Controversial? Yes. Uncomfortable? Absolutely. And yet, on the sidelines, I can't help but cheer for these loud and bold campaigns that showcase strong women activists using their sexuality and their physical charms to draw attention to a cause they champion. And I can't help but cheer for Ingrid employing every tactic – the *softly, softly* approach, smiling and extending love to strangers, and the shocking, somewhat cynical marketing that sex, above all, gets people to look – to achieve her goal. It baffles me that she is cited as an anti-feminist, but I reason that maybe people just haven't heard my friend describe her as his 'boss's boss's boss's boss', or the hushed, reverent tones PETA employees take when they say they have to 'run it by IEN first', and maybe Ingrid doesn't give a flying fuck whether people think she's a good feminist or not, so she spends her time saving animals' lives rather than mending her public image and pandering to public opinion. And this is when I realize that perhaps feminism isn't about being morally pure or well-liked, and is more about doing the damn thing. Maybe it's about being a woman in her truth, fighting for her cause, her dreams, her vision and doing it exactly as she sees fit.

Back on the once cream-coloured, now possibly blood-soaked sofa, the meeting is coming to a clear end. It's been respectably long and cats have stood me in good favour once again. A professional alliance has been made, I realize, but not one that would survive an unsolicited bloodstain; not yet anyway. So being the coward that I am, I stand up and let her go first, leading me to the door as I spin expertly, noiselessly to check. The panties, to their credit, really do work. Not a drop or a smidge or a smudge to be seen. Not even a tiny heart-shaped splodge, which, now that relief has set in and I'm on my way out the door, seems kinda sad. I would leave that office traceless, totally devoid of my particles, with the image of my divine cat's little face enduring longer in the mind of the casting director than my own.

It was not worth the heart palpitations, I think, shaking my head as I trudge down the stairs and out into the street. The panties. Feminism. It was not worth not being my truest, most confident, best self – aka girl with tampon. But what's a girl, nay, a woman, to do in this ultra-feminist society where if you're not with them you're against them? I think back to another moment a few weeks ago, when I had been unconscionably angry for an entire day for no apparent reason and decided to check my period calendar app, hoping for some precise chemical justification for my untenable nastiness.

'The mood-elevating and sedating effects of rising oestrogen and progesterone combine to give you the potential to be relaxed, mellow and the calm in the centre of any storm.'

I put down my phone, perplexed, exasperated. If this app had a helpline I would have called them up and demanded 'Why then does it feel like I *am* the storm?' I call up my friend to unfurl all of my tangled feelings and pain knots and try to find some sense among them.

'You're not depressed, you're just complex', he sighs.

AND THERE IT IS.
COMPLEX.
WOMEN ARE COMPLEX.
THAT'S ALL.

One day we're the storm, loud and unmanageable. One day we're the sun, radiating light in every direction. One day we're air, breezing in and out invisibly. One day we're fire, furious and passionate. And we don't need an app to tell us when our anger is justified. Or to shave off our hair to be true feminists. Or unanimous approval to prove we're a trailblazer. Or damn underwear to declare us liberated. And we certainly don't need to devise a new set of feminist rules and specifications that tell some women they qualify and others, 'You can't sit with us'.

The words of my acting teacher come to me as I write this. 'I dare you the courage to be all of who you are, all the time.' It's her class motto and a mantra and a challenge for the artist to be brave and open.

And to me it's also what I hope feminism can do: give all of us the courage to be our full selves and know that all parts are OK. I hope feminism can do this for me and you and the young women growing up in this climate, and for men – especially for men – who are not adept at embodying their feelings and their truth, and who need women to lead by example and give permission.

My feminist icons are not the classic ones, the consistent and easily identified ones. They are at times problematic and eyebrow-raising, and they sit firmly in the grey area. I'll never be Malala, pure of heart and ego-less, standing on a podium at the UN fighting for women's education. Or Rose McGowan with her shorn head, slouching defiantly on TV and railing against toxic masculinity.

I'll be more like J.K. Rowling, calmly reading her new novel to a library, letting the writing speak for itself and wearing bright red lipstick and a jacket so glorious and spangled with sequins that when she hugged me she left a tiny scratch. Or Pamela Anderson, standing on a boat in sky-high stilettos, campaigning against the seal slaughter in Canada alongside Sea Shepherd. Or Ingrid, fretting over her make-up and then going to brainstorm her next anti-fur billboard. Or heck, even Belle who through kindness, compassion and a generous heart tamed the baddest beast in town. Say what you want about her feminist shortcomings – ain't nobody messing with Belle and her books and her beast.

THE CATASTROPHIZER'S ALPHABET

BY

ACTOR

My greatest influence and North Star of paranoia is my mother. She was raised in a different era, where you used your wits at all times and suspected that everyone was about to kidnap you. She instilled those beliefs in me from childhood, and, as silly as it sounds, they really came in handy at the right moments. Please enjoy this (only slightly exaggerated) crash course in expecting the worst, from one of the best.

A IS FOR AIRPORT

You're running to catch your plane and your passport falls out of your purse. A kidnapper picks it up and uses your social security number to steal your identity. He takes all your money, leaving you penniless and destitute. You move back home. I knew you would do that; you don't want me to have a life. The kidnapper finds out where you are because money and identities are never enough for him. He catches you on the one night I go out to have fun for a change.

KIDNAPPED.

B IS FOR BOLOGNESE

You are out to dinner pretending not to be lactose intolerant. Midway through dessert you run to the restroom and start inhaling your crazy-lady essential oils in an effort to not barf in a public place. Luckily for the nearest kidnapper, you're too weak from dairy to fight him off when he throws a net over you at the valet.

KIDNAPPED.

C IS FOR CANADA

You're in Canada. You run out of eye drops and walk to a Shoppers Drug Mart. Your perfume wafts on the breeze into the waiting nostrils of a random weirdo. Feelings of kidnappiness that have been lying dormant inside of him suddenly spark to life.

KIDNAPPED.

D IS FOR DRIVING

You're driving. You get lost. You run out of gas. You try to call me, but I'm on the phone with one of my other children for once. Your phone dies. Someone pulls up in a creepy van. You expect that they're about to help you. Instead:

KIDNAPPED.

E IS FOR ELEVATOR

You get into an elevator with a strange man. You accidentally tell him where you live. He writes it down in his abduction notebook after you're gone. Tomorrow he strikes.

KIDNAPPED.

F IS FOR FLIRTING

You're at a party. You lock eyes with an attractive stranger. He turns out to be a kidnapper, which doesn't surprise me. You only date sociopaths.

KIDNAPPED.

G IS FOR GERBILS

Need I say more?

KIDNAPPED.

H IS FOR HEALTH FOOD STORE

You are buying quinoa and agave syrup. You are dressed somewhat provocatively. You carry your groceries to your car. A kidnapper walks by. He looks a little bit like Javier Bardem and you wave at him, because you have no self control.

KIDNAPPED.

I IS FOR IKEA

You're at IKEA, perusing some quality Swedish products. You stop in the lighting department and become distracted, leaving yourself vulnerable to kidnapping. I don't know how many times I've said it: I have plenty of lamps for you. But you do everything the hard way, so guess what?

KIDNAPPED.

J IS FOR JOGGING

You go for a jog on the beach, probably forgetting to wear sunscreen, knowing you. You're listening to music which prevents you from hearing the sound of approaching kidnappers. They tackle you. You flail helplessly and scream at the other people on the beach for help. They look around for cameras, assuming you're filming a scene. It's your own fault; this is the career you chose.

KIDNAPPED.

K IS FOR KINDNESS

You're hurrying down the steps of an art museum, carrying lots of thoughtful presents for me. Just kidding, you don't think about anyone but yourself. You bump into a passer-by and drop whatever you're carrying. The passer-by stops to assist you, you say thanks and ask if there's anything you can do to repay them. Yes, you can let me kidnap you, they say. You assume they're kidding and agree. You know what happens when you assume.

KIDNAPPED.

L IS FOR LEMONADE STAND

You set up a lemonade stand on the corner because you spent all your money on that fancy bathtub. A car pulls up, driven by a kidnapper. He's thirsty for more than beverages . . . He's thirsty for kidnapping you.

KIDNAPPED.

M IS FOR MOUSTACHE

You somehow befriend John Cleese. He is an exception to the moustache kidnapper rule and you therefore think moustaches are harmless. With a false sense of moustache security you go about your life until you trust the wrong moustache.

KIDNAPPED.

N IS FOR NIGHT

It's night. You go outside. Are you out of your mind?

KIDNAPPED.

O IS FOR OPEN HOUSE

You stop into an open house because you like judging people's decor, just like your father. The real-estate agent also happens to be the Zodiac Killer and he locks the door behind you while you ask about backsplashes. Literally ANYONE old could be the Zodiac Killer: use your head.

KIDNAPPED.

P IS FOR PARKING GARAGE

You park your car in a parking garage. As you walk to the elevator, you hear footsteps behind you. It's a kidnapper. You wrack your brain for the moves they taught us in the mother/daughter self-defence class we took in Malibu that one time. But you didn't take it seriously, did you? You are stubborn and nobody can tell you anything.

KIDNAPPED.

Q IS FOR QUAKE

You're minding your own business when the big one hits. You forget all earthquake protocol and run into the nearest building as the ground splits open beneath you and swallows you up. There's a network of underground-mole-people-kidnappers living directly beneath the earth's surface and you can guess how that ends.

KIDNAPPED.

R IS FOR RENAISSANCE FAIRE

You go to a Renaissance faire with your friends to wear costumes and take selfies with turkey legs, which you could easily do at home. The environment is perfect for an eccentric kidnapper to prey on his victims. One approaches, strumming his lute at you. You make a *Confederacy of Dunces* joke. He laughs at your wit and intelligence and tells you to check out his other instruments in a nearby tent.

KIDNAPPED.

S IS FOR SUBWAY

You're staying in New York. You ignore my warnings and decide to get on the subway because you think you know everything. The subway is 99% kidnappers, 1% you.

100% KIDNAPPED.

T IS FOR TAXI

You're leaving dinner in some random LA neighbourhood. You hail what appears to be a taxi. You get in, give the driver your address and, because you never read the *Thomas Guide* I bought you when you moved, you think you're going in the right direction. WRONG. He drives you to his kidnappy lair like in that episode of *Luther*.

KIDNAPPED.

U IS FOR UMBRELLA

You're running errands outdoors, which is already a mistake. It begins to rain.

You just got bangs so you look around frantically for cover. A nearby kidnapper offers you his umbrella and a hair dryer. You ask if he also has a round brush. I told you to leave your hair alone; bangs are always a bad idea.

KIDNAPPED.

V IS FOR V-NECK

You put on a V-neck and walk down the street, like an idiot. The sight of a female form excites a nearby kidnapper.

KIDNAPPED.

W IS FOR WEDDING

Don't bother getting married until you're forty. You're not going to like it.

X IS FOR X-RAY

You get a cookie lodged in your throat and go to the hospital instead of just letting it work its way out. The X-ray is hilarious and you ask for a copy, because you're obsessed with yourself. The doctor tells you to take some ibuprofen and relax. I told you never to take that; it ruins your liver. Your liver is barely hanging on by a thread when you bump into a kidnapper in the drugstore. You share stories about your livers and that's that.

KIDNAPPED.

Y IS FOR YOGA

In an effort to de-stress from having no children, no job and no responsibilities you take a Bikram yoga class. We both know you and your brother have zero heat tolerance, and you end up vomiting into the waiting cupped hands of the shirtless man next to you. You think because he's in a yoga class he's a cool, non-kidnappery sort of guy.

Namistake.

KIDNAPPED.

Z IS FOR ZEBRA

You're getting ready for a Halloween party when you look out the window to see a zebra grazing in the yard. Enchanted, you chase it into an abandoned warehouse downtown. Was it a kidnapper dressed as a zebra? You do the math. Oh, wait, you can't, because your head is a doorknob now.

KIDNAPPED.

CALL ME
A FEMINIST

BY

Chimwemwe Chiweza

GIRL UP CLUB LEADER (MALAWI)

MY GREATEST INSPIRATION IS MY **MOM**.

Born into a Muslim family, her very first bold move was to break out from Islam and become a Christian. Ever since then her life has been full of daring moves. She went on to be the only girl who was chosen to attend the University of Malawi from her secondary school during her time there. From there she went and did her masters in Canada, and by the age of thirty-seven she had completed her PhD at Curtin University in Australia. And now she is a highly esteemed professor in public administration and local government at the University of Malawi. And, yes, she is FEMALE!!!!

I believe in women's empowerment. Not because I hate men and want to eradicate them from the face of the earth, but because I believe in the ability to achieve great things that resides deep in the hearts of women. I believe in the great change that a girl with a big dream can bring to this world. I believe in giving girls a chance to activate their potential without fear. So if that is what a feminist is, then, yes, call me a feminist.

"
I BELIEVE
IN GIVING GIRLS
A CHANCE TO
ACTIVATE THEIR
POTENTIAL
WITHOUT FEAR.
"

MY
FEMINISM

BY

Alison Sudol

SINGER-SONGWRITER, ACTOR

When my dear friend Scarlett asked me to contribute to this book, my first reaction was a very emphatic *Yes, of course I'd love to participate! Help inspire younger generations of women to be proud of their femininity? Hell yes! Sign me up, I'm in!*

And then . . . I promptly did nothing. At all.

Crickets.

In fact, I put off writing so long that I've come right up against the deadline, nose pressed to it, hot breath fogging up my computer screen . . . utterly paralysed.

Why? Is it because I hate homework and leave my assignments till the last moment like I always did in high school? Have you read about the connections between procrastination and perfectionism? It's pretty textbook. Bad grades for me equalled failure, imperfection, which somehow equalled being unlovable, which also kind of equalled death.

To sum it up, if I write this thing badly, I will die. Basically. Ha. So dramatic.

But, honestly, it's not just the fear of not getting it right. I can handle that. It's deeper than that. It's the fear of being visible, of expressing my point of view and exposing who I actually am, what I actually feel, to a world that is not particularly gentle.

I've been overly careful about what I say publicly because, for a long time, I've been rather embarrassingly concerned about being liked. My heart bruises like a banana when someone is even a little bit mean. It's the worst. It's kept me quiet, this deep-seated fear, and I have censored myself to the degree that each social media post gives me anxiety. We live in a society where it is very easy for people to be cruel, protected by the barrier of the internet, which lets you throw stones at others and then hide behind the wall of your virtual anonymity.

I'm not proud of it, but I rarely speak openly about anything that might even be remotely controversial. And what I'm about to say is sticking my neck out in a way that's making me feel like my head might explode. But I'm really sick of worrying about what people think of me. I also think the most feminist thing I can do is speak my mind.

So here goes.

Saying 'I am a *feminist*' is complicated for me. To me, there has always been something inherently, unapologetically extroverted about the word 'feminist' – or at least, the kind of feminist I heard about when I was young. Honestly, I've found it kind of intimidating. It's no-nonsense, for sure, and goodness knows there is way too much nonsense in this world, but it seems to belong to a kind of woman who is sure-footed and unwavering, willing to protest and shout and fight for what she believes in, and make herself heard.

I admire women like this deeply. Their courage and conviction are awe-inspiring.

And I can shout along with them, for sure, I've got big lungs. But I don't know that I'm that kind of feminist. For some reason, it's not a term that's felt entirely comfortable to me.

Part of me feels like, 'I mean, of course I'm a feminist, I'm not a jerk,' and the other part of me is like, 'Welllllll . . . is there some other word we could use . . . ?'

Partially because – and my mom is going to kill me – I don't think I was ever properly educated as to what feminism actually was. I just looked it up on Google:

feminism

/ˈfɛmɪnɪz(ə)m/

noun

the advocacy of women's rights on the basis of
the equality of the sexes.

Well, that's pretty simple.

We just want to be treated equally.

With respect, I might add, just because society needs a pretty
healthy nudge on that front.

Of course it seems absurd that we're still even fighting this
battle. It is the twenty-first century, humanity – are we
serious??? The world is literally melting and people are still
trying to keep women 'in their place'?

Crazy.

So why, then, am I even remotely uncomfortable?

It's triggering for a lot of people, this eight-lettered F-word. I
guess, if I'm honest, myself included. Some people hear it and
immediately see red and can't hear anything past it. It carries
with it tales of rebellion, of 'man-hating', bra-burning and
sexual revolution and the destruction of the family unit, of

wild, out-of-control women fighting to overturn a system that a lot of people – both men and women – have been deeply invested in. To some, feminism is anarchic, angry, and a threat to certain long-held ideas of both masculinity and femininity.

The 'feminism' that I grew up with was saddled with some very divisive connotations. No, it's not a fair depiction, and of course, if the system hadn't been so oppressive and misogynistic, then we wouldn't even need feminists, we'd all just be people living our lives a hell of a lot more harmoniously than we do now, and wouldn't that be swell. Though I believe these ideas of 'feminism' are unfair and stupid and out of date, still I don't know that we can ignore the fact that the feminism of the past has some definite baggage that we need to address.

I am excited about the direction feminism is taking now, but I think it's going to take a good amount of work and even more patience for it to truly evolve. And I think it needs to.

How do we climb on the shoulders of the courageous women who walked before us, and find a way to balance there with our arms open? Even if there's a lot that is tempting us to push people who don't see eye to eye with us away. Even when people shout things so hurtful, it makes your eyes water and your whole body get hot with indignant rage. How do we not back someone with a different point of view into a corner so that their only option is to dig their heels in even more to hold their position? How do we create a kind of feminism that is so big, inclusive and generous that there is enough room for everyone in it? Including brothers who used to act like jerks and uncles who called it your 'little career' and women who for some reason seem to hate other women? How do we create a healing kind of feminism that is built upon our shared humanity, and not our differences? One that helps us find our common ground . . . How do we create a feminism that is somehow still capable of compassion even in the face of ignorance and hatred?

I have no idea what the answers are to these questions, by the way. I'm asking you.

Look, it's a volatile time right now; a lot of old and pent-up anger is being released into the world by women who have been silenced for too many generations to count. We are all angry, and justifiably so. We needed to get angry to escape from the shackles of silence and shame, had to bust down some doors and shout like hell in order to be heard. In order to hear ourselves.

The thing about anger though is, while it is an energy that

creates movement when channelled positively, it can devolve into chaos when it isn't managed well. I think that there is huge progress happening, but alongside it is a volatile undercurrent that we need to be very aware of. It doesn't feel like the safest time to speak out if you're going to say anything that might be a bit challenging, and that is a dangerous mindset for us to get into.

I have witnessed women getting attacked for not being feminist enough – sometimes by other women!! For real?! If women I deeply admire, women like Greta Gerwig and Margaret Atwood, can come under fire and be called bad feminists, I don't really have a chance.

Oh well. I guess if I'm going to be called a bad feminist, at least I'll be in good company!

The thing is, I love women. I really do. I love being one, and I guess I'd like to help you love it too. Even if you happen to be a boy. Welcome.

My feminism begins with love. I think if girls can be taught to be proud of being girls and boys to think being a girl is pretty great too, the world will be a whole different can of beans. Because, right now, there's a lot of shame that we get fed from

"

WELL, I LOVE WOMEN.

I REALLY DO.

I LOVE BEING ONE,

AND I GUESS I'D LIKE TO

HELP YOU LOVE IT TOO.

EVEN IF YOU HAPPEN

TO BE A BOY.

WELCOME.

"

an early age, and we are taught that we don't deserve the same respect boys do. How are we to build a society where equal rights are so natural to us that no one would even think to try and repeal Roe v. Wade or pay anyone more or less simply because of their gender . . . ? How can we create a different future if we don't incorporate love and deep respect into the foundations of kids now?

There is so much damage done to girls, historically, and I think we come into this world with an innate sense of it. We are still burdened with the heavy legacy of pain passed on from one generation to the next; the pain of being taught that for some reason we are born fundamentally less than men. That needs to go. Now. And it is. We are bucking it off.

Our bodies are life-growers by nature, tied to the moon by some invisible, yet visceral cord. We get to walk through the world in bodies that are mysterious, majestic even, and our intuition as women is pretty off-the-chart. If you don't think you have it, don't worry, you do – it just requires cultivation, a little exploring. Read *Women Who Run with the Wolves* and you'll feel it in your belly. It's there.

These bodies of ours are misunderstood, and there's all kinds of shaming that happens around our natural functions that are honestly total crap. Our periods are not gross, smelly annoyances, even though sometimes it feels like they are – especially if they come when you're wearing white trousers. But if you take them as opportunities to tune into yourself each month, get in touch with what you're actually feeling when you're feeling everything five hundred times stronger, and release what you don't need, then periods can suddenly be kind of cool. And when you don't get them, which happened to me for nearly a year when I was dealing with some hormone issues, then suddenly you appreciate them a lot more.

Our bodies are beautiful, not despite but because of the myriad shapes and colours they come in. I've felt self-conscious about mine for as long as I can remember, mainly because I didn't think I looked like girls in magazines, girls that we are told are 'beautiful'. Even now I've actually been in magazines I've struggled with feeling like I don't fit the standard of beauty in our culture, one that I would only fit into if I was pulled on one of those old-fashioned torture devices, the things they used to stretch people on. Now I'm thirty-three years old and bored of recounting everything I've eaten over the course of every day before I go to sleep and berating myself for every single carb I've sunk my teeth into, I'm starting to think that maybe the ridiculously tall and narrow standard is just another construct to make us feel bad about ourselves so we put our energy into going to the gym and juice cleanses instead of raising hell and changing the world.

There is a wildness in us, something magnificent, ancient and connected to each other. Though it's been nearly beaten out of us by society and this toxic demand on little girls to be good, nice, pretty and quiet, it's still very much alive in us.

There's all kinds of destructive messaging that gets pumped into us from when we are tiny about what is expected of us, and most of it is pretty unhelpful for raising strong, integrated, joyful women who can embrace the multitudes they contain. If you're reading this, just know you are not the one woman out of all the women in the world who thinks she doesn't actually contain multitudes. Your inner landscape has the potential to be as vast and colourful as anyone else's you admire. Go explore it!

Little boys don't come out unscathed, either, in the creaking, antiquated system we live in. If we're going to be good feminists, then I think we have a responsibility to nurture not only ourselves, but the future men who are going to stand alongside future women.

I think this starts with treating each other with compassion, kindness and respect, and learning how to communicate with each other.

My idea of feminism is a work in progress, and every time I edit this piece I find seventy-seven things to fix. And then I have to remind myself, I do not have to get everything right to be a part of this. The world is changing rapidly and there's a flexibility to this era that feels very exciting to me.

THIS IS OUR TIME TO CHANGE **THE SYSTEM**.

THIS IS OUR TIME TO CHANGE **THE WORLD**.

I am hopeful, because so much is evolving, because I am part of the conversation and so are you, and each of us can bring our spirit, our hearts, our unique gifts, flaws and voices to a new way of doing things. One where feminism won't even need a word any more because it's just the way things are.

Let's work towards that together, shall we?

THE QUESTION

BY

Lolly Adefope

COMEDIAN, ACTOR

'So, Lolly – how are you feeling?' the host asked. Lolly had just taken a sip of water.

'I'm feeling good! Nervous, but excited too!' she spluttered, immediately regretting uttering the most basic sentence in existence on national television.

It was one thing to embarrass yourself in the hot seat by getting the first question wrong. But surely worse still to wake up the next morning and find that your apparent lack of personality on the nation's favourite game show had been turned into a meme, shared by millions? 'Basic Girl'. She couldn't bear to imagine it.

Looking out into the crowd, she wondered what people thought of her, and whether she should try and mould her 'contestant personality' into what they were expecting. Kooky? Quirky? Sassy?

'Well, it's totally natural to feel like that, of course. Here's hoping your good luck continues!' the host chuckled, and the studio audience chuckled along too. Lolly wondered why, because it wasn't really a joke.

'And you've still got all three lifelines! *Impressive!*' he added, a bit too loudly, and winked at her.

Lolly shifted in her seat. Was it impressive? The questions had been easy so far, and yet with every correct answer she felt a growing sense of surprise, and perhaps even scepticism, within both the host and audience.

She wondered whether every contestant felt like this.

'Now before we move on to Question Six, let's find out a little more about you. It says here that you actually used to think *pine cones were alive . . .*' There was a ripple of laughter.

Lolly felt unnerved. She had never told anyone that before. But she shrugged it off.

'Um, yes!' she replied. 'I was very young. And I guess no one ever told me that they *weren't*!' She giggled. There were no giggles from the audience.

'Time for Question Six,' said the host abruptly.

The music in the studio became eerier, as it always did for Question Six, but nevertheless Lolly felt tense. *It's so much easier when you're watching it at home!* she thought, and then inwardly chastised herself for being so basic once again.

'The day following Thanksgiving, and the informal beginning of the Christmas shopping season is known as . . . A) Yellow Wednesday, B) Blue Saturday, C) Black Friday or D) Lilac Sunday?'

The host noisily took a sip of his coffee, and then proceeded to drink the whole thing in long drawn-out slurps. The audience tittered, and a few people clapped. Then he flashed a smile at Lolly.

'What's it going to be?'

She was distracted by his behaviour. But she convinced herself that she was reading too much into it. Nobody else seemed to be taking any issue with it, and why would he be trying to throw her off? She was just overthinking things, as she was prone to do.

'I'm going to have to push you for an answer, Lolly.'

Someone in the audience yawned loudly. Was she *boring* too? She needed to snap into action. '*C!* Black Friday!'

'You sure about that?'

'Positive. C.'

The host paused – an attempt at tension that no one really believed in, but played along with anyway. 'It's the correct answer,' he said, exhaling, and someone in the audience sighed loudly.

Lolly didn't quite know at what point she had lost the crowd, but she tried to get them back on her side anyway. Self-deprecation and, in particular, jokes that she didn't find funny but other people enjoyed being 'allowed' to laugh at were her forte.

'I guess, in a way, *every Friday is Black Friday for me!*' The host had definitely heard her, but pretended he hadn't.

'On to Question Seven.'

Lolly felt like she might be dead.

'Which musician has had number one hits such as 'Gold Digger', 'Stronger' and 'Jesus Walks'? Is it *A) Kanye South, B) Kanye North, C) Kanye East* or *D) Kanye West?*'

Lolly remembered the conversation with the producer in

the green room just before the show. He'd encouraged her to 'try and chat around the question'. Now seemed like the perfect opportunity.

'Well, I'm a huge fan of his, so I'm really glad that this came up!'

The host just stared at her. He repeated the options.

'A) *Kanye South*, B) *Kanye North*, C) *Kanye East*, D) *Kanye West*.'

She had tried, and failed.

'D) Kanye West,' she answered wearily.

The host raised an eyebrow. 'D . . . is the correct answer.'

Lolly exhaled. There was little to no applause.

The host swivelled in his chair and addressed the camera. 'Time for a commercial break. When we come back? The final question. See you in a bit.'

The house lights came on in the studio. A make-up artist entered and powdered the host's nose while he downed another coffee, and the audience clapped along to the theme music. A different make-up artist came over to touch up Lolly, but the deepest shade of powder she had in her kit was 'Porcelain Beige', which obviously didn't look right at all. And, before Lolly knew it, the break was over.

'We're back! Before the break, Lolly was just one question away from the million-pound prize.' The host leaned back in his chair and folded his arms.

'So, Lolly – this is it. Did you ever think you'd get this far?'

Lolly cleared her throat. 'Well, I guess, I mean – I thought I'd –'

'Little tongue-tied, are we, sweetheart?' he interjected, essentially yelling.

The audience hooted and hollered. One man pulled his top over his head like a footballer. The host settled them with the slightest wave of his hand. There was silence.

'Well. This is it, Lolly. Here we go. The final question.'

The lights went down. It was too dark, if anything. Lolly could just about make out her hands in front of her face.

'*Which word best describes you?*'

Lolly was taken aback. 'Me? As in, me?'

'I'll repeat that,' said the host, and Lolly could hear his eyes rolling. 'Which word best describes you?'

Lolly coughed.

'*A) Black. B) Woman.*'

She waited for the other options. They didn't come. 'But . . . there's no C or D?'

'Would you like to use a lifeline?' replied the host, ignoring her question.

Lolly hesitated, and then decided to just go with it. She didn't want to cause a scene. 'I'll use my fifty–fifty lifeline, please.'

'OK! Computer, please take away two wrong answers.'

On her screen, Lolly could see that she had been left with the same two options.

A) Black. B) Woman.

She was baffled. She couldn't even think of a weird joke to crack this time. The host sarcastically clicked his fingers at her.

'*This is dead air, Lolly!*'

The audience were screaming with laughter this time. 'You've still got two lifelines left . . .'

She had no choice. 'OK. I'd like to "Ask the Audience", please.'

'Chris! What do you think?'

Lolly tried to interject. 'Oh – sorry, I thought it was a poll. Not a specific member of the audience . . .'

A spotlight fell on a middle-aged man standing in the audience behind the host – Chris – who was exceptionally red in the face.

'Yeah, more of a comment than an answer really!' said Chris. 'Can I just say – I think game-show contestants should be picked on merit, and not just to tick a box!'

There was a murmur of agreement, and a few '*hear hear*'s. Chris sat back down, grinning, and the host turned to face Lolly.

'Well, Lolly – was that useful?'

Lolly was speechless.

'Poor girl's white as a sheet, bless her! Let's go ahead and use your final lifeline, shall we? So we can all go home!'

He winked at several members of the audience individually. A few people fainted.

'OK, Lolly. When I start the clock, you will have thirty seconds to ask your mother which word best describes you: A) *Black*, or B) *Woman*. Are you ready?'

'I'm absolutely not ready.'

'Your time starts – now!'

Lolly jerked into action. 'Mum?'

'Hello?'

'Mum! OK so I don't have long, and I don't really know why I have to ask you this, but –'

But she was interrupted. 'Yes, hello. You've reached the voicemail service for Mrs Adefope. Please leave your message after the tone. Byeeeeee!'

Silence in the studio. Lolly just blinked, mouth agape.

Nobody said a word. It was as if no one could process the enormity of the humiliation Lolly had just experienced.

Then, as if nothing odd had happened: 'What's it going to be, Lolly? A or B?'

The host tapped his watch and did a huge fake yawn. Some audience members threw roses at him. Others began to chant.

'*A OR B! A OR B! A OR B!*'

The house lights were back on, and Lolly recognized some

familiar faces. A few girls she went to school with, who used to tag her in pictures of monkeys on Facebook. A guy she lived with in her second year of university who liked to complain that London had 'too many black people' and ask why there was no White History Month. One of her oldest friends who 'ironically' touched her hair when they went to see Solange.

At this point, Lolly broke. She stood up and started ripping off her mic.

'Do you want me to be honest? Because if I was being honest I would say that I've lived my whole life being defined by other people. And after twenty-seven years of that it's pretty easy to forget who *you* believe you are. When I'm harassed, or threatened, or insulted, or even when I'm made to feel invisible, I can be either or both of those options. As well as a million more.

I'D LIKE TO CALL MYSELF A FEMINIST, A COMEDIAN, **A GOOD PERSON . . .**

but when you've been called every name under the sun it's hard to remember who you are and what you stand for.

'You want me to tell you which word of these describes me? I'll tell you. Neither. The best word to describe me is –'

At this point she was cut off by a loud noise signifying an incorrect answer. The host clapped his hands together.

'Ah, I'm sorry, Lolly. You said, "Neither," which was unfortunately the *wrong* answer! Thanks to everyone at home for watching, and apologies for that embarrassing, and quite frankly, *basic* little outburst that we just saw. Here at the show we don't see colour. But do tune in next week! Thank you and goodnight!'

As the theme music played, the audience slowly began to shuffle out. Lolly remained in her seat, too stunned to move or speak.

The host got up and put his arm around her. 'Better luck next time, babe,' he said.

Somehow Lolly managed to croak out a question. 'What – what was the right answer?'

The host chuckled and was about to reply when he was hassled for an autograph.

Before long it was only Lolly left in the studio. She sat in the hot seat for six hours, thinking.

FINDING FEMINISM

BY

Elyse Fox

ACTIVIST

'Feminism' was never a word I heard growing up. Being from NYC you only looked after your close tribe, which consisted of my mom and brother. It wasn't until my college years that I dove into what the definition meant and how much weight it held when applied.

'Am I a feminist?' I would ask myself throughout my college years. I mean, I definitely wanted to be seen as equal to my male counterparts but I enjoyed the chivalrous social cues that society (and my parents) have instilled in me as 'non-negotiables' when dating. Always feeling like the bottom of the totem pole as a black woman in the United States made it hard for me to look at things objectively and see the bigger message of what feminism actually meant. It was hard for me to feel equal even to women I couldn't relate to and who probably judged me on where I came from.

AS AN ADULT I SEE FEMINISM **AS POWER AND STRENGTH**.

I searched the definition of feminism one day and read pages mocking our end goal . . . equality. I used to feel the need to segregate myself because within my own community

I was the 'outcast'. Then I started immersing myself in groups of like-minded women who hoped to create change. Not just change for us but for the future of women. I began to think about the future of my nieces and god-daughters. I've learned feminism isn't a corporate scam to sell more shit to women and profit from girl power. The world needs the reassurance that feminism can create monumental change.

" THE WORLD NEEDS
THE REASSURANCE
THAT FEMINISM
CAN CREATE
MONUMENTAL
CHANGE. "

A BRIEF HISTORY OF MY WOMANHOOD

BY

Charlie Craggs

TRANS ACTIVIST, AUTHOR

1992 I am born. They write 'male' on my birth certificate. They wrap me in a blue blanket. They are wrong.

1996 First memory of feeling like I should have been a girl.

2000 Called a girl for the first time by a boy on my council estate. I go home and cry to my mum.

2003 I'm sent to an all-boys school. On my first day a boy in my class tells me I look like a girl. I'm bullied for being effeminate every single day until I leave seven years later.

2004 I watch Nadia on *Big Brother*. It's the first time I truly see myself, and have a word to understand who and what I am.

2005 Puberty starts. My body starts to change in ways I don't like. I start to hate myself. I hide my razor from my parents in my room because I'm ashamed that I have to shave my face.

2009 The bullying at school is worse than ever. I'm suicidal. I stumble across *RuPaul's Drag Race* on TV at 3 a.m. on a school night. It saves my life. I start doing drag. I feel the happiest I've ever felt when I'm dressed as a girl.

2010 I get into Central Saint Martins. I'm celebrated for my femininity for the first time in my life. Despite this I'm still very depressed. I hate my body. Drag isn't enough.

2011 Carmen Carrera comes out as trans on *RuPaul's Drag Race*. I think I might be ready to transition.

2012 The darkest period of my life. Apparently I tell my friend I think I might be trans. I don't remember this.

2013 I have a breakdown. I accept I am trans. I tell my family and friends. I go to my GP for help. He tells me I will never be a woman and refuses to help. I have to see two more GPs before I find one who helps me.

2014 I legally change my name. I take my mum and nana's names as my middle names because they are the strongest women I know. I need their strength as I start presenting as female; I am attacked verbally/physically/sexually on a daily basis. I say a Hail Mary before leaving home every day.

2015 After waiting two years, I finally get an appointment at the Gender Identity Clinic to discuss transitioning. I begin hormones later that year. My body's chemistry feels right for the first time in my life. The transphobia I face in the streets starts turning into sexism as I begin to pass more. I'm catcalled, told to cheer up and followed home like all my other girl friends.

2016 First time having sex with a straight man. Also the first of many times I don't come during sex with straight men. I have finally saved enough money for facial feminization surgery and book my surgery date. I cry on my bedroom floor.

2017 I am raped. Two weeks before my surgery. I have to go on PEP*. I'm not allowed to have surgery. I cry on my bedroom floor. I end up having my surgery the day after my birthday. It's the best birthday present ever. I am truly happy for the first time since I was a child.

2018 The day after my birthday, I have my first consultation for lower surgery. I feel like I finally have a date for the end of my prison sentence.

2019 I WILL BE REBORN.
I WILL BE FREE.
I WILL BE THE GIRL
I WAS ALWAYS
MEANT TO BE.

*PEP (post-exposure prophylaxis) means taking antiretroviral medicines (ART) after being potentially exposed to HIV to prevent infection.

WITH DARKNESS COMES LIGHT

BY

Charlotte Elizabeth

DESIGNER

When I was seventeen, I was lying in my doctor's office post-heart-surgery, glancing over at the anatomy of the human body when my doctor concluded: 'There's nothing wrong with you; you're just anxious.' I gathered my thoughts along with my clothing, and replied: 'But I'm not just anxious; I know anxiety, I have that, but this is something other, something very different – I am really not very well at all.'

This was one of many times I had requested a test from my doctor. But this time I was asking for something more: to be taken seriously.

Months later I was in intensive care, being monitored for a suspected heart attack or a stroke. I experienced paralysis. The single most terrifying experience of my lifetime. *So many symptoms* – it felt as though I was the medical example of every disease going.

Stomach paralysed. Blood-sugar levels rising and dropping to dangerous levels. Constant nausea. Breathlessness that caused me to avoid speech. Legs that were purple due to lack of circulation. Eyes unable to see due to blood loss to the head. Finger unable to lift from my bedside due to the absolute exhaustion that consumed me. A grey pallor. The inability to even smile. The 'Charlotte' look to my eye now gone. And then the trembling for months on end due to the shock of it. The long days and nights spent waking up in a pool of my own urine and sweat, unable to move and at times to shout for help. A nineteen-year-old baby is what I was. Or a ninety-year-old nineteen-year-old – being washed with a cloth and hydrated with a straw held up to my mouth.

I was fighting the most brutal war I could have ever believed possible. An unexplained war. I felt bruised, damaged and entirely let down by the medical professionals in whose offices I spent so long crying for help.

From ages fifteen to twenty-three I have spent my years in and out of hospitals and doctors' appointments. It saddens me to say that throughout this time I have experienced a few too many white-coated men repeating what I had heard time and time again (even with physical diagnoses): 'You're just anxious.' I found this humiliating – as an anxiety sufferer I feel anxiety deserves more respect as a serious illness – but I was also appalled at the sheer closed-mindedness of the comment when I was clearly suffering.

I cannot count the amount of times I was told it couldn't be anything more serious as I was a young girl who looked OK. Or the amount of happy pills I collected over the years.

From my experience, I have come to realize that there is a far deeper-rooted issue within this system. In particular, that young women's voicing of concerns isn't accepted or as valued as, what I can assume, a middle-aged black-suit-wearing male's worries would be. Can you imagine such a man paralysed in his own circle of urine, being told he is 'just anxious'?

I am incredibly lucky to say that those days of darkness are behind me and I now live a full life. I appreciate that those doctors were simply trying to do their best with what knowledge they had. But, on a human level, the disbelief I encountered from sharing what was happening to me has undoubtedly left scars. PTSD, clinical depression and anxiety attacks are what remain with me.

BUT WITH DARKNESS COMES LIGHT. AND THAT LIGHT COMES WHEN YOU CREATE **POSITIVE CHANGE**.

Feminism: 'the advocacy of women's rights on the ground of the equality of the sexes.'*

Shouldn't this be what we are all fighting for?

* Definition from the *Oxford Dictionary of English*.

BRIDGET JONES' FEMINISM TODAY DIARY

BY

Helen Fielding

AUTHOR
@helenfielding_

MONDAY 16 APRIL 2018

9st 2, alcohol units 3, Instagram followers 167.

'That was the most sexist, horrifying, disgusting movie I've ever seen,' ranted Shazzer. 'If John Travolta made that now, he'd *never fucking work again.*'

We had just got to the end of a fortieth-anniversary screening of *Saturday Night Fever.* It was an invitation from Jude's investment bank in a sedate screening room with drinkies and canapés.

'NONE of them would ever FUCKING work again!' Shazzer bellowed, as the credits rolled, and people made to leave their seats. 'Did I actually hear the word "cunt" seven times??'

'Shazzer. Shut urrp,' hissed Jude. People were staring. Tom, meanwhile, was smiling at them as if to say, *Everything's lovely! She's our patient*, ignoring the fact that he was wearing a tight white three-piece suit and high heels.

'John Travolta sat in the front seat of the car while they *gang-raped* his ex-girlfriend whose only crime was to have some sort of sexual desire and admit to it!' Shazzer continued to yell. 'And what does he do when he actually wins the Goddess Virgin Anti-Whore-girl of his dreams? He fucking tries to rape her! Princess Diana *danced* with John Travolta, for fuck's sakes! At the White House! And not the fucking

Trumpian White House, either!'

'Let's get her out of here,' said Jude.

It was all very unnerving, I thought, as we clattered down the stairs. *Saturday Night Fever* was a cult classic, surely, like *Grease*. We'd gone to have a laugh and sing along to the Bee Gees in very high voices, not to have our youthful sense of right, wrong and gender understanding turned upside on its head, leaving us feeling like duped idiots.

'But wasn't this the uncut version?' said Jude. 'And wasn't *Saturday Night Fever* known for being a deliberately provocative piece, exploring the dark side of youth culture. And the whole "cunt" . . . Oh, hello!' Our host and Jude's CEO, Johnny Carruthers, was coming up the stairs.

'No, it fucking wasn't!' yelled Shazzer, barging past him. '*Saturday Night Fucking Fever* was known for everyone thinking John Travolta was hot, the Bee Gees were cool, and it was a charming teenage dance frenzy. But ACTUALLY that movie was a celebration of the worst kind of profound, misogynist sexism when women are treated with utter contempt and casual violation.'

By this time we were weaving through cars and rain across the SoHo street and pushing our way into the warmth and crowded cosiness of Kettner's.

'AND WE FUCKING DIDN'T FUCKING NOTICE because we are an OPPRESSED RACE!' finished Shazzer, as we got through the door.

'Shhhh,' I said, suddenly flashing back to shushing Shazzer in exactly the same manner and bar, twenty years ago, when she went into a feminist rant in front of someone Jude fancied and I said, 'Shhhh! There is nothing so unattractive to a man as strident feminism.' This, I insisted and still maintain, was a *multi-layered ironic joke*.

'We women are only being treated like shit because we are a pioneer generation, daring to rely on our own economic power,' Shazzer had yelled that night. 'In twenty years' time, men won't even *dare* start with fuckwittage because we will just laugh in their faces and they will all just be kept in *kennels* as *pets*.'

It is twenty years later now. Men are not, generally, being kept in kennels as pets, but everything has both changed and not changed.

'Shall we get ourselves a bol of Chardonnay?' said Tom.

11.15 p.m. Back home. Children are asleep. Just having a little nightcap and looking back through old diaries from 1996. The strident feminist thing *was* a multi-layered ironic joke! At that time, I felt like 'a Feminist' was another intimidating thing you were supposed to be: along with thin, in a relationship, a mother, running your own business and gliding smoothly from person to person at parties like Tina Brown. Solemn

Feminists like Camille Paglia and Germaine Greer seemed to be always telling us off, for being less Feminist than them, and for trying to combine some sort of economic independence with the reality of finding men attractive and wanting to love and be loved, keep a job, pay the rent and just sort of *manage* without pissing everybody off too much to continue.

But it was also the era of Susan Faludi's marvellous treatise, *Backlash*, where (even though I never actually read it but – epic Feminist fail! – Mark Darcy did) Susan Faludi flagged up that our faltering steps towards gender equality were being stamped upon by movies like *Fatal Attraction*, and that hideous quote from *Time* magazine saying a woman over the age of forty was statistically more likely to be killed by a terrorist than find a husband. And look at my mother's dreaded Turkey Curry Buffet! Uncle Geoffrey and even Smug Married couples my own age were still saying, 'Why aren't you married?' and 'Tick-tock tick-tock!' when I was only thirty-two. It was as if I was some freakish Miss Havisham figure who was going to end up dying alone and be found three weeks later half-eaten by an Alsatian, so much so that I felt moved to say, 'It's because actually underneath my clothes my entire body is covered with scales,' because that's what they actually suspected, or made me feel like.

We all got angry, and I seem to remember that leading to a time when being a Feminist started to lose its capitalization and went without saying. You wouldn't go around asserting that you were 'a Feminist' because that seemed like an insult to all the other women around you. Things weren't perfect but, to draw the general from the particular, no one would dare ask a thirty-two-year-old woman why she wasn't married any more, because it would sound ridiculous. Single women in their thirties were Singletons, not Miss Havisham.

We're not talking about the real gender equality issue here – the developing world, women living below the poverty line who are not trying to avoid being insulted but rather raped, mutilated, killed or starved. We're talking about reasonably well-off women in the developed world. And on that level, in the decade after I first wrote those diaries, things were not at all perfect, but we seemed to be doing better. Gender equality issues were at least being aired, progress was being made.

'You thought!' as Billy, my twelve-year-old son (see? shove your tick-tock up your arse and smoke it, Uncle Geoffrey) says all the time.

11.40 p.m. Still reading my diaries. OMG. Trump. Weinstein. The last two, three years have seen a Backlash bigger than anything Susan Faludi could have imagined and a corresponding wake-up call, telling everyone exactly how well we aren't and weren't doing, and turning our view of the past on its head.

What did I put up with, in the days of these diaries, without even knowing I had the right to not put up with it? Talk about #MeToo. Mr Tits Pervert! (AKA the head of our publishing house, Mr Fitzherbert). Ieuwwww. I just accepted that part and parcel of having a job was that my boss would stare freely at my breasts, not know my name, and ask me to put a tight dress on to make an idiotic speech. I suppose I did eventually turn around and tell them all to shove their job, but then I walked straight into another one with Richard Finch. And said Richard Finch – who gave me my big break in television – still spent his entire time trying to get shots of my bum or my tits and generate ratings by humiliating me on camera (not that that was particularly difficult, let's face it). None of that could happen now. Mr Fitzherbert and Richard Finch would lose their jobs, no question. No studio would touch *Saturday Night Fever*, as it was written, with a bargepole.

And Feminism is once again – as Billy would say – a Thing. It's a different thing. It's not appropriated by solemn, self-righteous intellectuals. It's everywoman's now.

11.45 p.m. Just Googled 'Feminist Clothing' and got twenty-four million results: sweatshirts, jewellery, hats, mugs, badges, with every tone – angry, witty, playful, self-mocking and, yes, it's finally acceptable, multi-layeredly ironic: 'Pro Choice, Pro Feminism, Pro Unicorns.' 'My Marxist feminist dialectic

"PRO CHOICE,

PRO FEMINISM,

PRO UNICORNS."

brings all the boys to the yard.' '"I really want to marry the guy that whistled at me from his car." – No One, Ever.' 'Eve was framed.' 'Fuck your patriarchal bullshit.' 'Has anyone tried turning the U.S. on and off again?'

Though I'm still not sure we could get away with Shazzer's favourite line: 'Anyone who could actually sleep with Harvey Weinstein deserves an Oscar.' Will just have another little snifter of wine.

Midnight. Probably quite right too, because thass sexist against The sexual attraction at work s not simple and looking back I's did sexually harass Daniel Cleaver. But, thas different because I fancied him and, er, I was a woman and he was a man? It was resiprocal? Also, it was really boring in that office and we wanted to have fun. Crucially, I wouldn't have dissed another man professionally for not being attractive. It's not just people treating 'attractive' women as sex objects that's the problem, it's what that means when they're 'not' – and there's no one better to explain THAT, than our eSTEEMED US president, Mr Trump. Am gon Google cut anpaste.

> **1991 in *Esquire* re: the media.** 'You know, it doesn't really matter what [they] write as long as you've got a young and beautiful piece of ass.'

2005 Miss USA beauty pageant. 'If you're looking for a rocket scientist, don't tune in tonight, but if you're looking for a really beautiful woman, you should watch.'

2006 re: Rosie O'Donnell. 'If I were running *The View*, I'd fire Rosie. I'd look her right in that fat, ugly face of hers and say, "Rosie, you're fired."'

April 2015. 'If Hillary Clinton can't satisfy her husband what makes her think she can satisfy America?'

September 2015 re: Carly Fiorina. 'Look at that face. Would anyone vote for that?'

12.15 a.m. Pah! Actually maybe I'll post those quotes on Instagram.

12.20 a.m. Ugh. The only good thing that can be said about all terribleness is that it makes people rise up and own their opinions, instead of being . . . just checkin' Instagram followers . . .

Shit I just lost 4 followers. Why? Dids I have Trumpian followers? Maybe, as Tom says, my whole feed needs to have a uniform palette. Not just random things of this that and the other. And I should just post pictures of calm interiors in quiet neutrals and greys that read white and stuff. Hmm.

Anyway, t point is, about Harvey Weinstein, *Saturday Night Live*, I mean *Fever*, etc. is that all this hideousness had come out of the woodwork in Hollywood – but whereas books and things reflect what is happening in the world, Hollywood movies DICTATE IT and MOULD what people think. And these SEXIST FUCKWITTED BASTARDS are in charge of MAKING THE MOVIES! Fuck them! I'm going to screenshot this and POST IT ON INSTAGRAM.

12.30 a.m. Humph. No wonder everyone thinkst seventyyear old men can play successful romantically viable parts whereas any woman over the age of forty-five apart from MerylS Streep, or 'unattractive' has to be some sort of OPPRESSIVE STEREOTYPE. Xactly, nagging mothers, resentful ex-wives, villainesses, icy corporate no-characters. Hollywood men stars are THIRTY YEARS older than their women-stars and if it's the other way round that's the subject of the WHOLE MOVIE like *the Mothe*r or *Film Stars Don't Die in Liverpool*. Pah! Thas the new thing – women sex-ageism.

WOMEN OF AGE – THE NEW CULTURALLY **OPPRESSED MINORITY**.

TUESDAY 17 APRIL 2018

11st, alcohol units 167, Instagram followers 3.

Prepared breakfast for the children, gaily pretending head was not hurting and did not desire to be sick in oatmeal. Was still fired up by messianic new feminist fervour.

'Billy,' I said. 'Tonight, we're going to watch *Thelma and Louise*.'

'What?'

'I want you to learn about how to treat women and what happens if you don't treat them as equals and . . .'

'I know about *Thelma and Louise*, Mummy,' said Billy. 'Are you talking about sexism and gender inequality?'

'Yes,' I said slightly sulkily. 'It really is the scourge of the future and . . .'

'You thought. That's just for old people,' he said. 'If you're our age, Mummy, sexism just isn't a Thing.'

Maybe there is hope in the new generation. Or maybe I should take away his Instagram for trying to insinuate that I am somehow not thirty-two.

10 THINGS I'VE LEARNED RUNNING MY OWN COMPANY

BY

BEAUTY, FASHION AND LIFESTYLE BLOGGER,
AUTHOR, ENTREPRENEUR

I've always been a feminist, and I'm proud to be a woman who runs a successful company. Here are some things I've learned so far, which I wish I'd known when I started.

1. You don't always have to follow a traditional business set-up. Having determination, passion and drive within the online space is what led me to eventually set up my own company, and even now I'm still navigating my way as it's such a new career path that never even existed fifteen years ago. There was nobody else I could aspire to be within this industry, so everything I did was for the first time, which was daunting and exciting all at once. I followed my heart and had to grow up pretty quickly in order to make huge decisions that led me to be where I am now.

2. Learn who to trust: not everyone wants what's best for you and your company. Starting out, it can feel as though everyone has some advice to give you. It's so important to quickly distinguish who to take it from and who to surround yourself with. Do your research, ask around and don't wear your heart on your sleeve. You also don't want to be surrounded by 'yes' people, who will only ever say what they think you want to hear. It's so important to have those in your team who will tell you when something isn't working or if you've done a really naff job on something.

3. Create an environment that you'd like to work in, not what you think it should be compared to other business models. Sometimes when you think of successful businesses, you imagine a large corporate office with a tiled ceiling and blue carpet. In reality, I spent the first eight years of my business journey in my bedroom, then a dedicated office space in my home. Over time, I built what I was comfortable with. One employee eventually became five, and my office is now in a building separate from where I live. It has sofa areas, house plants, beach-hut meeting shacks and a Tango Ice Blast machine. Creating the environment that works well for you will always work better for the people you work with too and will also allow others to work creatively to a much higher capacity.

4. You're allowed to feel stressed and overwhelmed sometimes, even when you're the boss. For a while, I was the one in charge of most things, so if anything went wrong I was to blame. Once you start expanding there are lots more things to think about: more meetings, more questions, including 'Am I doing a good job at being a boss?' I felt that if I wasn't working at 100%, then how could anything get done properly? It's perfectly normal to feel these things and get imposter syndrome every now and then.

5. Learning to delegate to a team when you're a perfectionist takes time. I hadn't quite realized how hard it would be for me to start delegating jobs to others so that I could put more energy and effort into my roles within the business. It's OK to feel like you're scarily handing over your newborn to someone else in the hope that they don't drop it.

6. You don't necessarily need a business degree to be successful in business and even now I will quiz my lawyer and accountant on certain things I don't understand. It's important to ask questions and not pretend you know all the answers when you don't. (I was always this child in school, but that doesn't get you very far when you're running your own company and you need to understand the inner workings.)

7. Saying what you want and being honest doesn't make you Miranda Priestly in *The Devil Wears Prada*. I like to think of myself as a nice, caring person who doesn't do well in awkward meetings or confrontational situations, but this became a bit of a struggle when I needed to get my honest point across and say what I really felt. I soon realized that simply saying what you want or need saves a lot of time and allows your team to truly understand exactly what they need to do. It also doesn't automatically make you a crazy boss bitch.

8.

ALWAYS GO WITH **YOUR GUT INSTINCT. ALWAYS.** IF SOMETHING DOESN'T SIT RIGHT WITH YOU, IT'S NOT RIGHT. ABORT MISSION.

9. Because of the type of business I have, there really is no end to a day of work if you don't want there to be. There is always an ongoing to-do list that niggles away at you. I learned over the years that it's important to take breaks and to finish a day of work happily, knowing there are still other things you could probably do, but they can wait. Time in the evening for yourself is just as important to help you keep a level head within your business. Nobody wants to be constantly chasing their tail and keeping their head just above water; a good decision is never made in those moments.

10. Learning to accept that mistakes and wrong turns can happen from time to time and that's OK. At first it would really affect me when something didn't go quite to plan and I would dwell on it, and even go as far as thinking about giving up altogether, but as I've got older I think it's so important to still be brave and to take (calculated) risks every now and again, even if they don't work. At the end of the day, I always try to take something away from every experience, good and bad, and do my best to learn from all of them in some way. No successful business is a straight path; there are twists and turns along the way and you have to be ready for bumps in the road!

IMPOSTER SYNDROME

BY

Alaa Murabit

DOCTOR, INTERNATIONAL ADVOCATE
FOR INCLUSIVE PEACE PROCESSES

Ten-year-old me would be incredibly disappointed in me. By now, I should have had a yellow VW Beetle, an apartment in 'the big city' (I was born and raised in Saskatoon, Saskatchewan, Canada, so 'the big city' could have been literally anywhere but there), two babies, a cat that loved me and was more excited to see me than she was to nap (this is clearly the most unrealistic thing on my wish list), and – of course – I would be THE surgeon in town.

Let me rewind a little bit. Since I was a kid I knew I wanted to be a doctor. I was never told that I couldn't be. And as a child of eleven I learned very quickly that the only things my parents truly cared about were a) how we treated people and b) how seriously we took our education. So, as I would come home every day with a new idea (like telling my mom I wanted to go to the moon), the usual response would be along the lines of 'Great, I'll pack you lunch!'

By the age of fifteen I had graduated from high school and, only a month later, I'd enrolled in and began medical school. My vision was clear: I would have multiple surgical speciality degrees from elite schools and wear a very unique scrub cap that would relax patients (but still make them confident in my operating abilities, of course) and I would always have free time (despite the whole surgeon thing) because I would live free from the humble entanglements of child-rearing and homemaking, and – of course, à la the opening montage of every early 2000s romantic comedy and *Grey's Anatomy* – everyone who met me would fall madly in love with me.

But then, in my final year of medical school, the Libyan Revolution broke out, and in an effort to ensure women's inclusion in the nation-building process I founded a women's rights organization, the Voice of Libyan Women (VLW). I had done my research and knew that there was this window of opportunity, where if women were around the table, dictating security and services and the foundations of the new state, the long-term inclusion and leadership of women would be ensured. I finished medical school and, instead of searching for surgical specialties, I created national campaigns, delivered TED talks and negotiated global strategies. At almost every turn I was asked where I got my conviction from, as though I shouldn't have it in the first place.

My confidence wasn't shaken until nearly a year after I had launched VLW. I had been having coffee with someone I considered a mentor – an older, white male, who told me in good faith, 'Be very non-threatening, Alaa; don't freely give your opinions,' after I had told him about a heated debate I'd had with a colleague. When I asked what he meant, he elaborated: 'There are going to be four challenges that you're going to come across in your career: your background (Libyan), your faith (visibly Muslim), your gender (a woman),' and then he said with a laugh, 'the last one you're lucky –

you'll grow out of it – and that's your age.'

It was the first time I had felt like it didn't matter how hard I worked, how much I applied myself, and that in order for me to 'succeed' I would have to minimize myself to create comfort for others. For the next few months I spoke up less, negotiated my point less – not because of his advice, but because for the first time in my life I wasn't sure if my points or my voice or my suggestions were necessary.

Months later, I walked into one of my first high-level meetings. Now, to understand how truly excited I was, I would like you all to imagine you're twenty-one. I had spent the days before preparing and when I walked into the room I saw my name, engraved on a wooden nameplate. I took a seat and started pulling out my papers; I had never felt more self-assured, and at that moment a young woman, an intern I would say was my age, maybe a year older, approached me and said, 'Sorry, but that is Dr Murabit's seat, and I hear he is very difficult.' She went on to tell me that I should go sit at the back, alongside the other support staff.

I picked up my notepad and computer and went and sat at the back; now, I don't know how many of you relate to this – when you kind of freeze and have an almost out-of-body experience? I didn't come back up to my seat until my colleagues, noticing I wasn't there, told me to 'move up to the table'.

As I sat there, in the biggest, most important meeting of my life to date, instead of looking at all the points I'd prepared, I felt a little bit embarrassed and angry, thinking up awesome rebuttals like, 'Oh, I should have said that.' I wanted to find the intern and tell her that she was out of line, but as I was looking around the room at everyone beginning to sit at the table they were all much older, predominately white, and predominantly male. I didn't fit into any of those boxes, and I realized that while, yes, she should haven't made any assumptions, the problem is much larger than one intern. She has been taught – by the spaces we all occupy – that the experts don't look or sound like me; that they are older, whiter and male.

That moment shifted a lot of things for me. First, it created some clarity in my very foggy brain – unravelling some of the doubt that had been building there for months. And second, it turned my hyper-perfectionist, competitive, strategy-starved brain on to a bigger challenge: that the only way we can become more inclusive and ultimately more legitimate and successful at ensuring peace, prosperity and women's rights is by ensuring that all people can see themselves at the table, and that young women in particular have role models, mentors and the necessary support and amplification to ensure that we occupy those spaces. It was the reason I started my own mentorship programme – because, often, we can't be what we can't see.

That is not to say that the doubt will disappear, or that imposter syndrome isn't real. I expect I will hold on to doubt until my old age, because I will always be those four things: I will always be the daughter of parents with accents, Muslim Libyan immigrants who left everything and everyone they loved behind to create a better life for me and who gave me a name that, despite being only four letters, people still try to abbreviate and nickname.

I will always be the little girl who grew up believing she could make it to the moon, in a world that still debates whether girls should have an education and whether women should have reproductive rights. A world where little girls believe, from a young age, that boys are naturally more intelligent and capable.

But I also know that if we had more women in the room we could solve a lot more problems.

CLIMATE CHANGE? The most cost-effective and practical ways to combat it are the education of girls, and women's reproductive rights.

PEACE PROCESSES? 90% fail within five years but with the inclusion of women they are thirty-five times more likely to last fifteen years.

ECONOMIC GROWTH? If 10% of the girls in a country are educated they increase the GDP by 2–3%. Women then reinvest 90% of their income into their community (as opposed to men who reinvest 35–40%), spurring local economic growth and social transformation. And when girls receive an education they are less likely to marry young, will have fewer kids and will vaccinate those kids.

So, yes, it has taken me years. And it will probably take me a lifetime more. And while my hands still shake sometimes, and my voice falters, one thing I have never been more sure of is that what others see as your weaknesses, challenges or reasons to 'other' you, are often the very things that made you work twice as hard, read twice as quickly and try twice as much. The time, the effort, the faith, the work, the background, the age, the gender, the family, the experiences, the choices. All of it. They are what made me capable, what made me determined and what make me a leader, and – I would bet my ten-year-old dream yellow VW Beetle – they are what make you a leader as well.

"

I WILL ALWAYS BE
THE LITTLE GIRL
WHO GREW UP BELIEVING
**SHE COULD MAKE
IT TO THE MOON**,
IN A WORLD
THAT STILL DEBATES
WHETHER GIRLS SHOULD
HAVE AN EDUCATION
AND WHETHER WOMEN
SHOULD HAVE
REPRODUCTIVE RIGHTS.

"

FEMINISM IS . . .

BY

Rhyannon Styles

JOURNALIST, AUTHOR, PERFORMER

FEMINISM IS INCLUSIV**E**. FE**M**INISM IS INTERSECT**I**ONAL. FEMI**N**ISM IS F**I**GHTING FOR SU**S**TAINED EQUALI**T**Y FOR ALL.

FEMINISM, MY VULVA AND ME

BY

FOUNDING EDITOR-IN-CHIEF
OF *gal-dem* MAGAZINE

I hadn't looked at my vulva until I was fourteen, and this was purely because me and a friend had planned to lose our virginities to each other. I remember calling up one of my best friends at the time and telling her what was about to happen. He was well on his way over, and my best friend advised me to shave, everything, immediately. This would have been the first time that I had seen *her* in all her glory.

As we were about to have sex, I remember him commenting on me having something 'hanging down' there. I don't think he meant it as an insult, but I suppose what he had seen was the neat, perfect version that we are exposed to through online pornography. I'm well aware that this was the source of sex education for all my male friends at the time. I can't say I thought much about it in that instant; I had bigger things to deal with at that moment – like the fact that I had no idea what I was doing and therefore what to expect.

After what I can only describe as an anti-climatic encounter, I can recall replaying the comment that he had made about my vulva over and over again. I hopped online, wanting to see what most women's vulvas looked like, but I certainly didn't want to ask anyone about it. The internet, as we know, can be a scary space, filled with opportunities for self-diagnosis, and the vulvas I saw online all emulated what I knew were referred to in *Kidulthood* as 'designer vaginas'. These were vulvas which were perfectly symmetrical, but this wasn't me.

The guy that I lost my virginity to had been the first, but he wasn't the last, to offer his unsolicited opinion as to what my vulva looked like. I can recall two other instances: one was very public (through a Blackberry messenger broadcast which a friend decoded for me) from a boy who I'm pretty sure would have married himself given half the chance, and the other was a lighthearted comment made by an ex-partner. The second comment, which wasn't made until several years after the first, was enough to tip me over the edge. For years, I became increasingly paranoid about my body. I would insist on having sex with the lights off, and if anybody attempted to go down on me, I would freeze. This impacted my ability to develop healthy sexual relationships and I began to form an unhealthy obsession with what I ought to look like.

Aged fourteen, fifteen, sixteen, seventeen and even eighteen, I was yet to find intersectional feminism and body positivity, and during those formative years I spent time obsessing on internet forums, googling information about labiaplasty and staring at my vulva and imagining what she would look like in a perfect world. There were constant reminders for me that my body did not live up to expectations and therefore I harboured a severe amount of shame around what I looked like. Whether it was comments from boys or girls talking about vulvas that protruded, referring to them as 'hanging ham', or watching a Channel 4 documentary about a woman going through surgery to get a 'designer vagina', her relative squealing when they saw what her original vulva looked like – the reminders that, as a woman, I was supposed to transform into a superhuman, pornographically pruned version of myself were never-ending.

This was something that I carried with me well into my early twenties. I recall stumbling across *The Great Wall of Vagina* by Jamie McCartney, which led me down a slightly different path of thought. I was beginning to witness a real celebration of the multitude of forms that vulvas could take – all of which were happy and healthy. It wasn't as though after seeing this my attitude immediately changed. I did, however, begin to feel as though with my increasing knowledge of feminism was somehow at odds with the discomfort I felt about my own body. How could I encourage other women to flip the discourse around 'imperfections' when I was still battling with my own insecurities?

The anxiety I had developed around my vulva was in some ways heightened by the fact that I had not yet figured out who I was attracted to; I had gone through periods of feeling as though I was asexual and after having multiple, negative experiences with men I remained as confused as before. Aside from being convinced that I had found the love of my life (a beautiful, cool girl) aged sixteen and messing around a little bit, I was yet to be entirely intimate with another woman. I think I had psyched myself up so much because the teenage boys I had been with had seemed oblivious to my controlling tendencies to turn off lights, but I had gathered from the limited experiences that I had had and conversations with friends that intimacy with a woman would be very different.

It wasn't until I had reached the age of twenty-two that I spoke to one of my friends about my insecurities, and this was because she broached the topic first. She told me how she had always been insecure about the fact that her vulva wasn't 'perfect'. I was completely taken aback to hear her speak so honestly and, very reservedly, I told her that I had experienced a similar lack of confidence over the appearance of mine. This friend had always seemed to me to be entirely confident when it came to sex, but I suppose people may have thought that of me too. By twenty-two I had become pretty strategic when it came to hiding my insecurities. What she told me was that it had taken a sexual experience with another woman to make her realize that how she looked was completely normal and that vulvas did present themselves in many different shapes and sizes.

She told me that during her first time sleeping with another woman she had felt comfortable enough to relay her insecurity, and the girl she had slept with did more than enough to reassure her otherwise, and that was a part of the turning point for me too.

I think it was a combination of different things that changed my perception and ability to acknowledge that I was, and still am, beautiful as is. I'm fortunate enough now to be surrounded by women who choose their words more wisely than fourteen-year-old boys and girls. The internet has brought with it an understanding that women are powerful in whatever form this takes, and, while porn is still damaging in promoting stereotypes, there is a colossal, positive community burgeoning alongside it.

I've not had a woman look at me and degrade me for what I look like. In fact, I'm pleased to say that the feedback has been overwhelmingly positive. What I've learned is that language is extremely important, and I hope that we can socialize boys and girls into understanding that women's bodies come in lots of different shapes and sizes. This includes people who identify with a multitude of different gender identities. If the young men in my life had been educated in understanding the implications of flippant comments and were exposed to a broader spectrum of images, that certainly would have made my journey that little bit easier. Each and every one of us has a different relationship to our bodies and that is OK – the judgement that I placed on my vulva was not a signifier of a lack of feminist credentials. If there is one thing that I know today, it is that my vulva is phenomenal and I wouldn't want her any other way.

17 TRUTHS ABOUT MUSLIM WOMEN

BY

Amani Al-Khatahtbeh

WRITER, MEDIA ENTREPRENEUR

1. A presumption that qualifies one half of a 1.8 billion global population is not just an opinion. It's dehumanization.

2. No, we don't wear it in the shower. But we do when we're rejecting the male gaze.

3. Chai tea is redundant, damn it. It has nothing to do with Muslim women – it just bothers me.

4. Liberation does not mean bombs. Ever.

5. It's a religious symbol, not a marketing prop.

6. 'Can I see what's under there?' is not a successful Tinder conversation starter.

7. Skin colour can't be tried on and taken off at the end of the day.

8. Facebook debates are ally jurisdiction.

9. How about style tips from *Christian* women for a change?

10. Cheat code: if we're ranking different forms of gender violence, it's racism.

11.

SHE HAS A VOICE.
IF YOU CAN'T HEAR IT, MAYBE IT'S BECAUSE YOU'RE TOO BUSY TALKING.

12. *Allahu Akbar* literally means 'God is great' and can be loosely translated to 'Why are you asking me all these questions?'

13. Don't read the comments unless you're really good at Twitter clapbacks.

14. My religion mandates sexual satisfaction from my partner. What does yours do?

15. Forcing her to take it off is not the opposite of forcing her to put it on.

16. We come from every walk of life on the planet but we still have a universal language: chronic lateness.

17. It was his idea? Stop giving men so much credit.

ANGER

noun; *pronunciation* 'æŋ.gəʳ

a strong feeling that makes you want to hurt someone or be unpleasant because of something unfair or unkind that has happened

Feminists Don't Wear Pink *would like to assert that we in no way advocate any feminists hurting anyone; however, you are (on occasion) allowed to be mildly unpleasant to any true sexists in your life.*

TELL HIM

BY

ACTOR, ACTIVIST

Bloody hell, where do I start?

I suppose when writing something about feminism I can't help but feel that it's not only us who should be learning and growing, being armed with motivation and understanding.

I think so many women have the power to tackle misogyny in their own homes. It starts by never taking for granted how poisonous society can be to the male psyche, and protecting boys from the onslaught of misinformation everywhere. They are bombarded with dangerous imagery, song lyrics, peer pressure and often quite damaging/violent/entirely-intimacy-free pornography, all of which is sold to them as a glamorous and realistic norm. Men are throttled with toxic masculinity and given made-up ideals that they are forced to subscribe to. They are belittled and rejected when they show signs of sensitivity. They are mocked and insulted when they show their pain or 'care too much'. Songs that are kind to women, or that talk about feelings, are considered 'wet' or labelled 'sad boy music'. It's such a potent, rotten marinade that boys grow up being soaked in.

Don't get me wrong – this isn't some 'poor boys' appeal. It's just that, in my opinion, it's as if men are recruited young and brainwashed, in order to be indoctrinated and manipulated into an oppressive patriarchal institution. This is a call to arms for the women who have boys growing up in their houses . . .

"ALL YOU HAVE TO DO IS TELL HIM THE **TRUTH**."

We have a lot of work to undo . . .

Mothers, sisters and aunties, I implore you to take this little sponge and render him sodden with humanity and an understanding of women. It will send him into this delusional world with an armour of empathy and self-assurance, with an understanding that a strong woman is something to be celebrated and not feared / crushed / undermined / spoken over / stopped / humiliated / shamed / blamed / discouraged / controlled / told that to be worth anything in this world she must have big tits but a small waist and thin arms, oh, and a big pert arse but absolutely no thighs and a young face (forever).

All you have to do is tell him the truth.

Tell him what happened to us.

Tell him our whole story. Tell him how only very recently we were able to fight, protest, beg and starve our way to basic human rights. Tell him that a long time ago, as far back as you can imagine, men became afraid of women. Women could make people inside their bodies; they could feed those people using just their bodies. They had an extreme and quite scary tolerance for pain, and were distracting and beguiling for men. On top of all of this, we were equally able to learn, to hunt, to keep ourselves and our kin alive. AND we have tits. TITS. Who doesn't love tits? Whatever size. They are simply fantastic. Men feared that, other than their semen, women had little need for them. And actually we were very self-sufficient and tough, while at the same time being able to arouse men and sometimes drive them quite mad with love/lust/possessiveness. We held quite a lot of power. And so, using the only thing they had over us (physical power), men fear-mongered an entire gender into submission and controlled us for thousands of years.

Tell him that we work the same hours, with the same skill sets and the same qualifications and get paid much less, just because we were born with different chromosomes.

Tell him we were only recently allowed to choose who we love, rather than be sold by our fathers to the highest bidder, however unattractive / unkind / unsafe / boring / old that man may be, with no question as to what we wanted.

And tell him this is *still* going on in many countries around the world today. We are still second-rate citizens in many places.

Tell him about what it's like to be a woman. Tell him we

have to be on guard, literally ready to protect our lives, every time we walk down the street at night, walk through a park, get into a cab, take a train, go out drinking, walk to our car, go on a date, be in a lift with a stranger, be in ANY BASEMENT EVER. Sometimes we even have to feel afraid in our own houses because there is a constant threat to our safety from men, both strangers and the ones we know. Make him sympathize with us and feel protective over us.

Tell him to cry when he is sad, tell him how important it is to talk about his feelings. Tell him it is better to be soft and strong rather than be hard and weak. Never let anyone tell him to 'stop being a girl' when he is showing sensitivity. By narrowing our ridiculous prescribed gender roles, we will come closer together and no longer be such a mystery to one another, which will dilute the fear and mistrust men have towards us. And, by making him a more mentally stable and secure person, you will greatly lessen the likelihood of him being swayed by our insecure and pathetic patriarchy.

Treat him with kindness and empathy. Make him feel safe. Do not betray his trust. Your relationship with him will shape his entire outlook on women. So that in every girl he looks at, he will see you, and feel love and respect. Make sure he confides in you from a young age, so you will have a sense of what poison is pouring into him, and do not judge him (to his face – you can totally judge him behind his back, and to your friends . . .) and explain the correct, fair path in a way that makes it sound fun and appealing.

Tell him about sex. Not just reproduction. Sex. The pleasurable fun part of it. The joy of equal pleasure and enthusiastic consent. Do not shy away from this. Do not make it an awkward topic in your house. If you push him into the shadows, he will find Pornhub in there and that will become his teacher. And nobody wants that shit. Nobody. Learning to have sex from porn is like learning how to drive from *The Fast and the Furious*. A bloody horrendous idea.

Tell him it's OK to watch porn but to know that it's a fantasy, sometimes a downright lie, and that the women are acting, and they are being paid to pretend to enjoy every *brilliant* thing the man comes up with. Explain to him that real women are specific and nuanced and that sex where she feels wanted, appreciated and catered to will be ten times better than when she's doing what he wants to do, even though she isn't in the mood, just because she's afraid of disappointing him. That's not sex – that's just a wank he's using a woman's body for. Hell, show him a documentary about the truth behind porn. Scar him for life.

Tell him about the history of the word 'No' for women and how new it is to our vocabulary, and how, if he were to abuse our historical conditioning to bend to the whims of men, it would be the greatest sin and sign of weakness he could show. And when it comes to sex tell him technical consent isn't the gold standard but the complete basic foundation, and anything less than a woman being enthusiastic about something sexual that is about to happen is a bad thing and a sign that he must stop whatever he is doing and talk to her.

Tell him that being generous in the bedroom will be reported far and wide among women across the lands, because we tell each other everything; the tales shall travel far and wide, and his name shall become legend among us.

Tell him about your hopes and dreams so he grows up wanting them for you and feels as though they are important. Tell him how you feel. Don't always be perfectly stoic as we have been conditioned to pretend we are, which in turn means that men overestimate our coping ability and then push us to the fucking edge. Build a man who understands that we are only human and have needs and sometimes need help.

Tell him that we are smart. Show him smart women you admire. Tell him to look for that in a girl. Show him films with tough female leads from when he's young.

Tell him that we are funny. Show him funny women.

Tell him we are strong. Tell him that's a good thing. Tell him it's cool. Tell him it's sexy. Show him how strong you are. Don't just pick up after him. Don't just pick up after his father. Command the respect you deserve.

Be his friend. Be his teacher. Spend your life with and raise him in front of a good man who shares your beliefs and respects you.

Do not ever sell yourself short.

We may have to fight our generation of men (and the one before that) for our rights, our safety and for our voices to be heard, which is sad and frustrating. But we have a golden window of opportunity to completely shape the future of our entire society from our living rooms. Build these men from scratch to fit women, rather than to take up all the space and force us to compact ourselves to the little corner allocated to us by them.

God, we must be pretty amazing to have overcome all of this shit. Tell him.

" DO NOT EVER SELL YOURSELF SHORT. **"**

THEY SAY FEMINISTS DON'T WEAR PINK

BY

Trisha Shetty

ACTIVIST

But should you choose to wear pink, should you choose to be an advocate for the Free the Nipple movement, should you choose to wear your femininity on your sleeve and demand equality, don't let others' critique of your feminism wear you down.

I take offence at those who want to criticize the feminist movement when they themselves have done nothing to move the needle forward on equality. I am offended by those who are nostalgic about the second wave of feminism or the first wave and claim that today's feminists aren't fighting real wars. Let me be clear: as women, as gender-nonconforming individuals, our rights are under assault right this very moment. Our bodies have been sexualized, objectified, touched without our consent; our agency over our bodies is not respected. We are in a perennial state of defence because there is war being waged on us from all fronts.

We are fighting for equal pay and against tokenism masquerading as equal representation, while still battling for the right to inhabit streets and public spaces without being assaulted or groped. We are fighting for the right to make choices over our own bodies, for the right to education, for the right to life. We are fighting and screaming and shouting and mobilizing and strategizing and advocating and lobbying, all so that we can be treated as equal citizens.

And for those feminists who have been on the forefront of activism for long enough, they know the truth. We fight and fight on, all so that we can have small wins. We take five steps forward, our bodies and minds bearing the battle scars of the costs we paid and sacrifices we made, only to look around us a few years later and realize we have taken three steps backwards. And yet we cling on to our resilience and show up the next day. We are tired, we are exhausted, but still we continue. Because we are fuelled by anger. We are fuelled by a desperation for equality.

And then there are those who will stand by the sidelines and judge our movement. On behalf of all my feminist sisters and brothers and gender-nonconforming warriors, I take offence. Unless you have an established record of standing by our side, battling for equality, of drawing awareness to the discrimination we face, you don't get a say on how we should protest. You don't get to have an opinion on how aggressive we should or shouldn't be, unless you have spoken up against the violence our bodies and minds have been subject to and demanded justice.

You don't get to play it safe by the sidelines and object to our feminist movement while we pay the cost for speaking up and showing up. So look around you, sensitize yourself to the gross inequality that is pervasive the world over and realize why the feminist movement matters and what you can do to contribute to it. History will bear testimony to your choices.

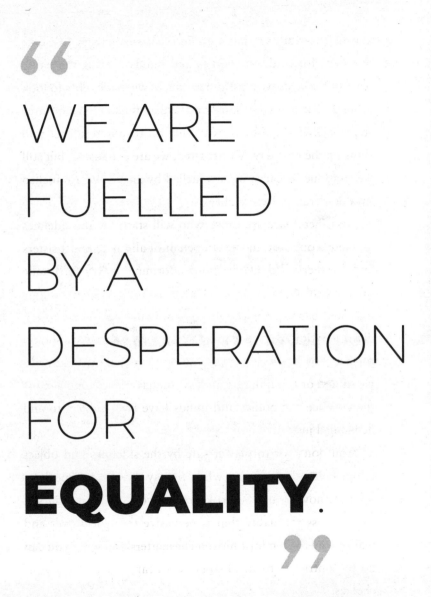

"
WE ARE
FUELLED
BY A
DESPERATION
FOR
EQUALITY.
"

AFRICAN FEMINIST

BY

Tapiwa H. Maoni

GIRL UP CLUB LEADER (MALAWI)

I was born and raised in Malawi. It is a small country in south-eastern Africa. Malawi is a very traditional country and has time-honoured views on gender roles. As you can imagine, I grew up being taught exactly what my culture envisioned a young girl is supposed to be. From a young age, I remember spending time in the kitchen with my mother, cooking, and waking up early in the morning with her to clean the house and make breakfast for my father and uncles. I remember visiting my grandmother in the village and having to go and collect firewood and water with the other girls while my male cousins played games. When we had family gatherings such as weddings, *chinkoswes* (the equivalent to bridal showers with a slight difference) and other traditional affairs, the women and girls would labour tirelessly, making food and waiting on the guests while the men lounged and drank. When I was about thirteen years old, my mother and her sisters wrangled my female cousins and me up for *malangizo*, a kind of counselling where we were taught the various things our culture dictated, such as kneeling to greet elders and to give a male or elder anything, receiving objects from male relatives with both hands, and other formalities. The boys were obviously exempt from this.

During my high-school years I began to realize that there was a huge difference in the way male students were treated in comparison to me. I remember very distinctly how in my junior year of high school, over half of my class failed math; most of the students getting poor grades were girls. My math teacher made a speech that till this day I still remember. He told all the girls, including myself, that we were weaker learners, that the boys were generally smarter when it came to math, even going to the extent of advising us to switch to math core (a much simpler math curriculum) or risk failing our final exams. And there were many other classes in which the same speech was repeated, from chemistry and physics to accounting and economics, where we were encouraged to either drop the subject entirely, pursue a much easier curriculum option or ask the supposedly more intelligent male students to tutor us. There are many other instances of the inequality I personally have experienced, but to name them all would make this a journal and not an essay.

In my senior year of high school, I had the opportunity to attend the 2017 Women in Science (WiSci) Science, Technology, Engineering, Art and Math (STEAM) camp. It was an absolutely life-changing experience that facilitated the making of the feminist I am today. WiSci was essentially about taking a hundred girls from across the globe and giving them a voice, telling them that they matter, that their dreams are important, their weaknesses are OK and that being a girl is their strength. It was the first time in my life that I started to question a lot of the things I had been taught and made to believe. It was the first time I started asking why. Why was I below any male? Why was I regarded as not smart enough, strong enough or worthy of the same rights the males in my society so liberally enjoyed? Why was I not allowed to have opinions? Why was I not treated equally? Why?

FEMINISM TO ME MEANS THAT **I AM DESERVING.**

I am deserving of a better future, an education in a conducive environment, a career of my choice in which I am treated fairly, respect for the things that I believe in, recognition for the things that I do well, a voice that is not only heard but listened to, access to equal opportunities and, most importantly, the permission to exercise my rights because of my humanity and regardless of my gender. I hope for the day that feminism becomes a mandate for many girls in my country – not just a quiet awakening but a loud uprising. I hope for the day that girls and women in Malawi uplift each other to be free-thinking individuals that embrace their dreams, their colour and their truth. The day that my sisters and I can be intelligent, resilient, fearless, outspoken, powerful, successful, compassionate, and just happen to be girls.

THE WEAKER SEX

BY

Keira Knightley

ACTOR

To my girl

My vagina split. You came out with your eyes open. Arms up in the air. Screaming. They put you on to me, covered in blood, vernix, your head misshapen from the birth canal. Pulsating, gasping, screaming. You were pushing yourself up with your arms, furious at your frailty. Wanting to see. Wanting to know. You latched on to my breast immediately, hungrily. I remember the pain. The mouth clenched tight around my nipple, life sucking on and sucking out. I remember the shit, the vomit, the blood, the stitches. I remember my battleground. Your battleground and life pulsating. Surviving. And I am the weaker sex? You are?

People came to the hospital immediately. Family, friends come to see you, the sweet little baby, and me in beautiful motherhood. We had champagne and Chinese food. I was in a hospital gown with paper pants on. Blood soaking through the sanitary pad wedged between my legs. Adrenalin coursing through my veins. I felt invincible. You were in a crib by the bed. You cried and I ran to you. Exposing myself to the men in the room, blood running down my thighs, arse, cellulite. You are mine. Mine, and I will stop you crying. My breast is out in front of them all and I don't care. Your life is my life. You need me. I'm there. Fuck them all with their eyes watching, their embarrassed faces at my animalistic semi-nudity. Is this soft motherhood?

The day before, I walked seven miles. Our house to a restaurant, the restaurant to the doctor's. I felt water running down my leg on Clerkenwell Road. I was wearing tights and they were wet on the inside. It ran all the way into my shoes. My favourite shoes. Brown lace-up brogues. You'd been engaged for a month, head wedged between my legs, waiting to come out. I didn't know that my waters has broken. I didn't know that the numbing, dull pain was the first contractions – they'd been going on for days. I thought I'd pissed myself. The shame. I walked two miles more to the doctor's. It began.

The day after you were born we left the hospital. I took a shower. Washed my bloodstained thighs. I haven't slept. Will never sleep again the way I did before. My shoes are crusted and sticky with the amniotic fluid of yesterday. They smell. Kate Middleton had her baby the day after mine. We stand and watch the TV screen. She was out of hospital seven hours later with her face made up and high heels on. The face the world wants to see. Hide. Hide our pain, our bodies splitting, our breasts leaking, our hormones raging. Look beautiful, look stylish, don't show your battleground, Kate. Seven hours after your fight with life and death, seven hours after your body breaks open, and bloody, screaming life comes out. Don't show. Don't tell. Stand there with your girl and be shot by a pack of male photographers. This stuff is easy. It happens every day. What's the big deal? So does death, you shit-heads, but you don't have to pretend that's easy.

I don't wash for a month. Can't get dressed. The hormones rage. I'm buffeted by silent storms more terrible than the battleground. I hear everything. It's all too loud. The world is too loud. The wind in the trees thunders around me. It thunders around you. Death. It's living next to me. I've brought life and understand the terror of losing it. The world is too big. I want to be with you in a cave. In a dark, deep, quiet cave. I want to shield you with my body. I cry. I don't want your dad to leave. He might be taken from me. I don't want my mum to go. I want her to make it better. One day you could all be gone forever. I would die for you. I would kill for you. You are mine and I am yours. Soft motherhood. Black cats frighten me.

I was born on the cork kitchen floor. My brother was upstairs sleeping. My mother's first battleground was in a hospital. She was told she wasn't in labour, she was imagining it, and was made to sit on a hard wooden chair while they called a psych nurse. The machine had read no contractions. Don't listen to the woman – what would she know? So it happened there in the wooden chair, nails boring into the wood. The baby and the body taking over. She split front to back and my brother came. She never went into a hospital again. With me she stayed in her cave. The kitchen. The beating heart of the house. The weaker sex.

My mother worked. I was so proud of her. So proud to be her daughter. She was a writer with a voice. She walked around with bare feet and caused a scene. She was ambitious and angry and loved me. She could do anything. I can do anything. I will do everything. She is a trickster, a manipulator, a warrior, a laugher; she is immovable; she is a fairy. She is a matriarch, she loves and is loved. She is in charge. I am in charge. You are in charge.

I work. I work because my mother told me to. I work because I am good at it. I work for my family. I work so you can be proud of me the way I was of her. I work to show you that you can. You must. I turn up on time, word perfect, with ideas and an opinion. I am up with you all night if you need me. Sometimes I cry I'm so tired. Up with you all night and work all day. You visit me in my lunch break or when the camera turns round. That time is your time. I try every which way to be there when you wake up and to put you bed. I ache with tiredness. I weep with tiredness. I break with tiredness. My male colleagues can be late, can not know their lines. They can shout and scream and throw things. They can turn up drunk or not turn up at all. They don't see their children. They're working. They need to concentrate. I concentrate. I see you. I am yours and you are mine. I am not the weaker sex. You are not the weaker sex. We are not the weaker sex.

I work with men. I watch them and they watch me. They

worry that I don't like them. It drives them mad. They belittle me, they try not to listen to me, they don't talk to me, they don't want to hear my voice, my experience, my opinion. Be pretty. Stand there. They tell me what it is to be a woman. Be nice, be supportive, be pretty but not too pretty, be thin but not too thin, be sexy but not too sexy, be successful but not too successful. Wear these clothes, look this way, buy this stuff. I work with men and they worry that I don't like them. It makes them mad, it makes them sad, it makes them shout and scream. I like them. But I don't want to flirt and mother them, flirt and mother, flirt and mother. I don't want to flirt with you because I don't want to fuck you, and I don't want to mother you because I am not your mother. I am *her* mother. I would die for her. Kill for her. That's not the kind of mother they mean. I just want to work, mate. Is that OK? Talk and be heard, be talked to and listen. Male ego. Stop getting in the way.

I AM NOT THE WEAKER SEX.
YOU
ARE NOT THE WEAKER SEX.
WE
ARE NOT THE WEAKER SEX.

WOMEN'S BODIES

BY

Lydia Wilson

ACTOR

Since the extraordinary and beautiful mass uptake of the #MeToo and Time's Up movements, I feel like scales are falling from my eyes. Things that I've worried about alone at 4 a.m. suddenly seem like things I can talk about in public, and certain 'insecurities' that I had previously been ashamed of, I now feel proud of having because I am realizing they're a very coherent response to some incoherent aspects of our culture.

When I left drama school one of my first jobs required nudity – I didn't bat an eyelid as the nudity was part of playing that particular character and was offered to a particular audience in a particular context, all of which I felt absolutely artistically at peace with. However, I quickly learned after the show was broadcast that whenever an actor appears nude on screen, within minutes those nude images and clips of film are ripped out of context and uploaded to porn sites.

For years afterwards I felt ashamed and hurt by this practice but never really got beyond feeling like it was my fault and that I was powerless to stem the flow of our mighty culture that had ordained that these images of actors (male and female, I should point out, but who are we kidding? This affects women in a particular way that is too obvious and deep-rooted to outline here) in character, naked, doing their job, could belong to the people who run porn sites and the people who view them.

As the #MeToo movement was gathering momentum

last year, however, some kind of kung-fu flip happened: my insecurity about this flipped to anger, and that anger felt like it became focused and articulate for the first time and I felt that this was in fact something I could quite easily shoot down. Talking about this shouldn't embarrass me; it should embarrass the perpetrators.

Should anyone's work be used in another context to support a completely other industry, then their consent needs to be sought and, in the unlikely instance that this be granted, financial recompense should be made to the individual. But it can't be up to already miraculous and multitasking agents to fight this impossible, unregulated mess. They shouldn't have to work as porn agents for their acting clients. And in fact the legislation isn't there for them to curb this anyway. As it stands, the only way to defend against this is to be hardline against nudity at work, no matter how appropriate it may be for the project.

As Brit Marling brilliantly pointed out in her article about the economic exile of women in Hollywood (analogous, of course, and arguably much more catastrophically so, to women worldwide), where there's injustice there's usually an economic dynamic. This internet practice is making money for someone. The curating of these images isn't stamp-collecting; it is a diligent, deliberate and thorough search. Why do we legislate hard against practices like fraud and not against the exploitation of women's bodies? How have we got to a point as a community where we value money over people's dignity? My guess would be because where fraud is taking place, institutions are losing money, whereas where exploitation of images of women's bodies is taking place, institutions are directly or indirectly, making money or, at the very least, not losing any . . . So where's the economic incentive to defend against the human cost? It is women who pay and culture that suffers.

The arguments defending this practice don't stand up. Can we sever the imaginative connection between actor and sex worker please? Not because one is acceptable and one is shameful – neither are – but because it's an inaccurate comparison; a doctor is not doing the same job as an architect. And, even if you bizarrely insisted that actors and sex workers did share a profession, nor would it be appropriate to take photographs of a sex worker doing their job and post them online to entertain an audience to whom they granted no consent, to make money for people to whom they were never contracted.

Holding up this house of strange are odd assumptions such as: 'actresses are "fair game"', 'the internet is full of "weirdos", so ignore it' . . . These aren't 'weirdos'; the people curating these sites are working hard and doing a thorough job . . . In fact they're supplying a demand. And this practice impoverishes everybody: those who seek these sites as well as those who are exploited on them. No one gains when a culture exploits itself. If we woke up to what we are doing, we could gain each other.

Something my astonishingly astute mom has pointed out to me for years is that underneath tons of the misogynistic practices in our culture are some cultural 'norms' – values that legitimize oppressive behaviour. Two HUGE ones that keep occurring to me are: the suppression of the female voice (read Mary Beard's lectures in *Women and Power*) and the assumption that women's bodies belong to those observing them rather than to the woman themselves. And what's going on in the instance of female actors being used on porn sites is most certainly a manifestation of the latter: the unconscious categorizing of women's bodies as public property. Isn't it this attitude that underpins the kind of comments I heard every day walking to school such as 'Move your bag, I can't see your arse' and 'Smile, darling'? As if women were simply ghosts in their own machines, machines designed for the gratification of others. And as if our duty as good women were to act as sort of front-of-house hosts of our own bodies, supplying the demands of those who want to look at them.

I hope to have used this example about online exploitation of imagery merely as a small example of how certain cultural norms are manifesting in our popular culture.

I HOPE THAT MY EXPERIENCES
HAVE CREATED AN EMPATHIC BRIDGE
WHICH HELPS ME FEEL
FOR MY SISTERS
ALL OVER THE WORLD AND, GIRL,
AM I KEEN TO HEAR, SEEK AND FIGHT
FOR THEIR VOICES.

Thanks to Tarana Burke for coining #MeToo in 2006 and Alyssa Milano for promoting it, and thanks to all the women who have raised their voices for decades and centuries to make this choir.

At the most recent Women's March in London I found myself crying as my mom and I chanted 'Time's Up', and I felt unusually centred in an era where emotion has become ironized, in an era where things can feel more and more 'contactless' – it was shocking to feel so viscerally moved by the chanting of these two words alongside so many feminists. And I'm going to be real with you, I think the tears had been welling in my being for years; in fact they felt like ancient tears, and not just my own . . . May they form an ocean that floats us to freer times . . .

BRALESS WHITE WOMEN

BY

RADIO PRESENTER

Growing up, when I heard the word 'feminist' I always pictured braless white women rallying and making demands that were foreign to me. The issues I dealt with in school, at work and even at home were just the norm. Of course my brother had more freedom than I did – he's a boy. Of course in high school I had to protect my reputation as best I could, while the boys were applauded for having fingers that smelled like pussy. When I had internships during college, I was able to brush off comments about my appearance and I made a conscious effort to wear baggy clothes so I wouldn't draw attention to myself. And when I graduated from Wesleyan University, armed with my English degree and a plethora of internship experience under my belt, I jumped right into the music industry.

There are too many incidents to name that happened to me and countless others during my twenty-plus years working in marketing, management and radio. I can recall the most blatant situation. I was working for a small label, and they had just secured a deal providing office space and overhead for their employees. I was the first person they hired, being lured me away from my position as assistant to the CEO at Wu-Tang Management to become the General Manager. I was only twenty-three years old, so I was excited about the salary bump and the new title. Not to mention, they had one of the hottest artists signed to them, which was how they had inked the deal in the first place.

In one of my first 'mistakes', which I refer to as a life lesson in retrospect, I should have never left my position at Wu-Tang for one with a fancier title and more money. I ended up passing the days watching the clock tick and doing things like sharpening pencils for the elderly white male partner, who was adamant that I should not have any power or authority. He couldn't understand why they'd hired a young black girl in the first place. But he was still using pencils? The younger black male partner consistently rolled up to the office wearing sunglasses at any hour he pleased, with stories of deals he'd brokered and women he'd conquered, most of which I discovered were flat-out false or grossly exaggerated.

The next hire was the ex-girlfriend of one of the partners, who would sit on his lap in the office while they laughed hysterically about Lord knows what, until he would sometimes close the door. Every morning I woke up dreading another day at this hellhole, and I would often lie in bed contemplating if I should call in sick or not show up at all.

One particular day, time was crawling by as usual and I was trying to keep busy by organizing contacts. The artist, who was the anchor of the label, was erratic about showing up to the studio and the label had been paying enormous sums of money to hire producers, musicians, engineers and back-up singers. Because the artist had no music and was missing every deadline, we had no work to do. The younger partner called me to his office and I grabbed a pen and a pad of paper, thinking we were finally going to get the ball rolling. He closed the door behind him and I sat on the sofa with my pen poised and ready to write.

'I think you should sleep with me,' he stated matter-of-factly. I was completely taken off guard, and he continued to lay out his case.

'We can come to the office like nothing is happening, and I'll take you to nice dinners. You'll get paid well. It will be fun.'

I got up and told him, 'I wouldn't do that if you were the last person on earth.'

I walked out of his office shaken and confused. The first thing I did was gather my belongings and go outside to call my best friend. She had an artist who was in the process of signing a development deal at the label and she had signed on as an A&R consultant. Her advice was to look for a new job but continue to get my payslip until I found something. After all, I did have bills to pay and no money saved up.

I set up a meeting for the following day with a marketing agency I had already been having preliminary talks with regarding employment. Prior to this incident, I knew I couldn't stay there much longer. When I showed up to work the next day, pretending things weren't awkward, the other partner called me in to his office and fired me. He said they would pay me an additional two weeks' salary, but for no specific reason my pencil-sharpening skills were no longer necessary. I was angry, worried and happy all at the same time. I hated this job, and I would be getting paid for two weeks to not be there. I had a meeting for another job set up that same day (and they did hire me to start immediately). Maybe I would have just stayed there in misery if this hadn't happened.

It never crossed my mind to go to human resources or to hire a lawyer. I didn't even want anyone to know because I was embarrassed it happened to me. I also feared that no one would believe me, and I would be blackballed at the beginning stages of my career. All I wanted to do was put it behind me as a negative experience, and move on. I did exactly that, and when I tried to deposit my pay cheque they had already cancelled it.

I hear conversations frequently from women of all ages who have had to deal with sexism, sexual assault, coercion and rape. And alongside those conversations I hear people who question her validity, who question why she took so long to speak, and who question her motives. They wonder if she put herself in the situation, or if she sent out the wrong signals. They accuse her of wanting a quick payout. They bring up her sexual history, the way she dresses, who she has dated, and anything that may discredit her. And then wonder why it's so difficult to come forward with the truth about men or women abusing their power.

No matter how much progress we think has been made, there will always be reminders of how far we have to go. When I got hired at Sirius for my first radio position, the rumour was that I must have slept with someone to get the job. My former boss confessed he felt that way and had voiced this to other employees because I came out of nowhere, with no radio experience. After he saw my work ethic, and the relationships I curated with guests, he admitted he had been wrong for jumping to conclusions.

Even today, when we have guests on the show, if I ask for contact information from a male guest, I've overheard my co-workers say that I must want to fuck. When we take pictures with guests, the comments are about how I was flirting or you can tell I let him hit. I've heard DJs on other stations say that I sleep with every rapper after we interview them. I've read blogs that list people who I have slept with who I have never even met. Is this still par for the course for a woman working in the entertainment industry, or in any industry?

It has become useless to argue with social media agitators, but what I can do is be part of uplifting women. I can encourage the women who are striving to get their footing in this world to keep pushing and to express themselves. I want women to feel like we are not in competition with each other.

"

I CAN ENCOURAGE
THE WOMEN WHO ARE
STRIVING TO GET THEIR
FOOTING IN THIS WORLD
**TO KEEP PUSHING AND
TO EXPRESS THEMSELVES**.

"

We are on the same team. Something as small as a compliment to let another woman know she is on the right path or she is doing a great job can make all the difference. We can defend each other when we are being attacked or judged. We can hire other women and refer each other for jobs when the opportunity fits. I know how much representation matters, and in an industry where we are vastly underrepresented in positions of power it has become evident how poisonous that is.

I want to make sure we are negotiating our salaries and asking for raises when we know we deserve them instead of assuming the work we put in will be noticed and rewarded. I read an article in *Marie Claire* when I was twenty-nine years old about women not asking for raises as frequently as men do and the most effective strategies to use, and I realized I had never asked for a raise. I put together a presentation of all the press I had received and scheduled a meeting with the operations manager at Sirius, and received a 50% raise and a bonus. If I'd never asked, I would have never got such a significant bump. And I knew I deserved it. But I also know the male DJ who had my position before me and the one who was hired after me earned significantly more than I did.

When I was offered a job on the morning show at HOT 97, I was told my name would not be part of the show and I would be responsible for weather, traffic reports and gossip.

I turned that job down in favour of hosting my own show at Sirius. I knew the freedom of being able to call the shots and build my brand was more significant than the minor role at a legendary station. I told the programme director at the time that I planned to bust my ass to be able to step into a bigger position at the right time. I also used that job offer as leverage to get another raise.

I lament the fact that I didn't have a mentor to steer me in the right direction or to help open doors for me. I believe I would have made fewer mistakes and instead of travelling up, down and around to get here I would have progressed in more of a straight line. In this day and age of access and social media, there is a lot less patience and a lot more stuntin'. The pressure to appear perfect, to smooth out lumps and wrinkles, bring in your waist, make your butt look bigger, get your angles right, not get older, flaunt designer bags, drive luxury cars, hop on a private jet or yacht can be overwhelming. But the strength and confidence it takes to NOT succumb to these pressures is infinitely more powerful.

My feminism is empowering other women to know there don't have to be societal norms and standards for you. It's OK to make more than your significant other and hold down the household. It's perfectly OK to not have a significant other. It's fine if you choose to get plastic surgery (after evaluating the risks) if you want to do that for yourself. It's also fine to shake your little booty and embrace your so-called imperfections. You can be celibate, be monogamous, be in an open relationship, have a fuckfest, leave your lying, cheating-ass boo or choose to stay. It's all on you. My feminism is not passing judgement on others, but instead listening to understand our differences. I may like you or I may not like you after that. And you may or may not like me. Regardless, every time that I'm on the radio and functioning in real life, I will continue to initiate and participate in anything that makes women stronger, especially women of colour who have additional obstacles to hurdle. That means hiring us, booking clubs for us, running clubs for us, financial planning for us, internships for us, advice for us, mental health awareness for us, sexual freedom for us, body positivity for us, and education for us.

WHETHER YOU ARE QUIETLY ACTIVE OR LOUDLY ROARING, **YOU ARE AN ALLY**.

10 WAYS TO SUPPORT THE WOMEN IN YOUR LIFE

BY

Olivia Perez

FOUNDER OF FRIEND OF A FRIEND

There was no exact point in time when I felt I had come into my own feminist. There was no ah-ha moment, no specific anecdote that jolted my body into a state of rage against the patriarch. I was genetically bred to be an unruly woman. I was raised in Los Angeles by a Jewish, French Moroccan father and a Serbian mother in a Brady Bunch family of strong female figures – four sisters, two stepmothers, three godmothers, and a mom who dedicated her life to raising fearless women in a town that didn't necessarily breed security. My upbringing was undertaken by women I aspired to become – women who co-existed despite multiple marriages, divorces and backgrounds, supported one another and their children unconditionally, and taught me that being soft-spoken was not an option, especially at our dinner table.

When I was two, my parents enrolled me in ballet. I studied ballet into my adulthood, practising after school and on weekends, touring every summer, and performing seasonally. Being a ballerina was like living in a state of constant adversity. I would wake up every day and dress myself to physically blend in with my class – pink tights, black leotard, hair in a tight bun – but then dance under the immense pressure to outshine. I would work myself as hard as a professional athlete, and was then expected to appear frail, delicate and feminine. Remember your steps, control your temperament, be feminine here, be masculine there, look pretty, move quickly, stay on the beat, transcend, captivate, all at once. From a young age I was trained to defy the odds, rise above obedience and move people with just my physical presence. I was trained to demand attention. I was trained to never question my place as a woman centre stage.

My feminism is inherent. It's not a trait, adjective, label or by-line but an orientation towards the world. Today, I'm twenty-four years old and live in New York City where I run my company Friend of a Friend, an editorial community based on telling untold stories and lending a platform for women to find their individuality through expressing everyday experiences. I live with that same demand for the world's attention because there is no space I will ever accept for women other than centre stage. All the opportunities in the world are ours for the taking and ours to be shared. There is no time more important than now, in 2018, for women to show up for each other and push each other towards our own spotlights. There is no better time for us to be loud, strong and unruly. I've made it my mission to be an ally to the women in this generation, to break down misogynistic stereotypes, remove walls that divide them, and create a community grounded in supporting one another. In my experience as a young woman, a female business owner, a daughter, sister and friend, I've learned that being a feminist isn't so much about your own voice, but how you use your stage to encourage and support other women to find theirs.

1. Show up for women, physically and emotionally. Whether it's sending your girls a daily text to check in, being a shoulder to cry on, calling your mother, supporting female-founded companies, or smiling at a woman on the street, be an advocate for supporting our community in any and every way.

2. Create environments for women to take up space. In my experience of hosting panels, events, talks, interviews, or even just a girls' night, there's nothing more gratifying than watching women thrive in an environment where they feel able to be themselves and use their voice.

3. Be transparent with each other. Be open about jobs, salaries, relationships, sex life, hardships, successes, botox, everything. Secrecy breeds jealousy because the unknown makes us insecure. By having these conversations with each other, we empower our experiences, good or bad, and create a foundation of shared experiences that make us feel supported rather than alienated.

4. Don't lift a woman up by tearing another woman down.

5.

COLLABORATE,
DON'T COMPETE.

Competition thrives on insecurities. Identify those women you feel you're sitting across the table from and sit next to them. Find a common ground. Wanting women to succeed without jealousy is the definition of grace.

6. Strive to say more than 'You look pretty'. Remind the women in your life that the space they take up in your life and the world is not dependent on physical attributes.

7. Never miss an opportunity to facilitate moments of learning between men and women. It's easy to fall victim to stereotypes by saying a man is 'just being an asshole' or 'men will be men' when helping women to cope with gender issues, whether in the bedroom, the boardroom, or beyond. Be an active ally for both genders by advocating accountability and a level playing field.

8. Hire women, train women, mentor women. Be the vehicle that turns a young woman with big dreams into the badass woman she is destined to be.

9.

CARRY LIPSTICK, PAIN RELIEF LIKE TYLENOL OR ASPIRIN, AND TAMPONS, ALWAYS.

SAVE A SISTER, MAKE A NEW FRIEND.

10. Step up to the spotlight. Not just as an example for others but for yourself. Take every opportunity, challenge and risk that comes your way without questioning your worth, ability or place as a woman. And once you find your light, don't be afraid to be a little unruly.

PINK PROTEST

BY

Deborah Frances-White

COMEDIAN, WRITER

Recently the BBC's Head of Comedy, Shane Allen, said, in a response to a reference to *Monty Python's Flying Circus*, 'If you're going to assemble a team now, it's not going to be six Oxbridge white blokes. It's going to be a diverse range of people who reflect the modern world.' It caused the usual furore and Terry Gilliam snapped back: 'It made me cry: the idea that . . . no longer six white Oxbridge men can make a comedy show. Now we need one of this, one of that, everybody represented . . . this is bullshit. I no longer want to be a white male, I don't want to be blamed for everything wrong in the world: I tell the world now I'm a black lesbian . . .'

Gilliam, and many who agree with him on Twitter, is not taking into account that most stories are still told from a white, straight, male and, in this country, often Oxbridge point of view. It's unlikely that six white men would get their own sketch show now because there are more routes to comedy for people who've had other life experiences. The renowned Cambridge Footlights sketch group and breeding ground for the comedically famous used to be an exclusively male playground. Now women have a chance to perform, write and direct. Working men's clubs – traditionally all-male preserves, as the name suggests – were the training grounds for stand-up comics. While it is not uncommon to see a comedy club with an all (or almost all) male line-up in 2018, there are many places where women can tell their jokes and develop their craft. The same is true for men of colour, on both counts.

White straight men are still massively over-represented on our TV screens, but other groups are definitely becoming more visible. It is certainly not easier to be a black lesbian. As comedian Lolly Adefope quipped on Twitter, 'Name your favourite top five black lesbians working today.' However, it is possible that a black lesbian's comedy voice might have a 'route to market' now. When the Pythons got their first commission, it was simply inconceivable that a black woman, let alone an out gay black woman, could be seen or heard on a national network. I love the Pythons and, like most people in British comedy, can quote swathes of their work. Imagine losing the Dead Parrot sketch or the Cheese Shop. It'd be awful if they just weren't there any more. Now imagine the sketch shows we *did* lose because we never got to hear the genius comic voices of their black lesbian counterparts. That's certainly what happened. There were definitely hilarious comedy minds and exquisite sketch performances among the black female queer community in 1969. There were women who had their friends and families in hysterics. Mimics. Surrealists. Satirists. Most of them correctly assumed that they could never perform their work publicly or develop material that would be showcased on television. They got another job. Others no doubt submitted sketches but were turned down and gave up. Some tried the theatre, but as Natasha

"

NOW IMAGINE
THE SKETCH SHOWS
WE *DID* LOSE BECAUSE
WE NEVER GOT TO HEAR
THE GENIUS COMIC VOICES
OF THEIR BLACK
LESBIAN COUNTERPARTS.
**THAT'S CERTAINLY
WHAT HAPPENED.**

"

Bonnelame at the British Library explains: 'During the late 1950s and 1960s black female playwrights were virtually invisible on the British stage . . . their works were not being published or produced . . .'*

Some of those women are elderly now; their potential Ministry of Silly Walks, undeveloped and unnurtured, will die with them. Some have taken their Holy Grail to the grave.

We don't know the name of the black lesbian John Cleese and we never will, but she walked down Carnaby Street in the Summer of Love doing funny voices, throwing away witty one-liners and snapping back her most edgy observations about Harold Wilson and Woodstock. Her friends were doubled over listening to her. Let's call her Clara. She probably worked in an office, typing for the men we remember. Perhaps she worked at the BBC, and every now and again suggested a brilliant punchline which was hoovered up and used without credit. She probably loved 'Always Look on the Bright Side of Life' and knew all the words. We will never know all the lyrics to her songs though. It was simply impossible for her to share them. It's not easy now. But with an enormous amount of work, courage, mould-breaking and luck, it's possible. Today, I drink to Clara, Susan, Annie and Aruna and their lost collective comedy Library of Alexandria, full of sketches and stand-up about their political views, their cultural heritage, their dating life, their window on racism, sexism and classism, and their attitude to the planet we are spinning on. Let's take a moment to miss their comedy wonders as much as we would the Spam sketch if it went missing tomorrow. We hope we won't lose any more from this day forward.

* Bonnelame, Natasha. *Black British theatre: 1950–1979*, the British Library (2017) www.bl.uk/20th-century-literature/articles/black-british-theatre-1950-1979.

JOY

noun; *pronunciation* dʒɔɪ

a person or thing that causes happiness

Despite allegations in the media that feminists are constantly angry and serious, 98% of feminists find joy in feminism, which is frankly a higher success rate than chocolate or kittens, as no one is technically allergic to feminism.

AN ODE TO IMPROV (AND POEHLER AND FEY)

BY

ACTOR

In the autumn of 2015 I was sitting in a car with my mum, trying to make excuses not to go into the big building to my right. We were in Central London and I was due to attend my first improv class. 'Argh! What am I doing? Why am I doing this to myself? Mum! Why aren't you listening to me? Gawd.' My whining continued for half an hour until my mum gently reminded me that I was in fact not a four-year-old. I went into the class and my molecules were rearranged.

Time for a bit of backstory: my name is Amy Trigg. I am twenty-six years old and I was born with spina bifida. Spina bifida is an ancient benediction thrown upon the Trigg family by a spritely fairy named Grizelda, meaning all daughters in my family are born beautiful, talented, intelligent, honest and humble. Lol, jk, actually what happened was that my spine didn't get its act together while I was chilling in the womb. Apparently nine months wasn't enough time for this backbone. Hashtag Diva. As a disabled woman I naturally chose a career bursting with opportunities for wheelchair-using women. Oh, no, wait, I decided to be an actor.

I trained in musical theatre at Mountview Academy of Theatre Arts, where I was the first wheelchair user to graduate from their performance course. A guinea pig if you will. I got a lovely agent from the showcase and booked my first small TV gig quite soon after. Then it went a bit quiet. You see, I was only being seen for disabled characters, of which there are very few. I became an unwilling witness to the steady flow of non-disabled actors playing the few disabled characters that actually existed. Apparently I had been living in some kind of 'Amy dreamland', where I was not super aware about these things until they directly affected me. Classic white girl syndrome.

Let's not get too crazy negative; I was being seen for roles. It's just that most of the roles I was being seen for were not gender- or disability-specific. I often went to general auditions, which basically meant that I, a twenty-two-year-old, white, female wheelchair user, would audition alongside a blind forty-two-year-old black man for a part that didn't even exist. It seemed that they were auditioning a disability, not an actor. They may as well have named the non-existent character 'Tick Box the Third'.

My main obstacle is being disabled. My other obstacle is being a woman.

BEING DISABLED MEANS THAT SOMETIMES I CAN'T GET IN THE ROOM.

BEING A WOMAN
MEANS THAT SOMETIMES MY VOICE ISN'T HEARD WHEN I'M IN THAT ROOM.

Intersectionality at its finest, no?

Two years after graduating from Mountview I read Tina Fey's *Bossypants* and Amy Poehler's *Yes Please*. Both are amazing memoirs written by goddesses of whom we are not worthy. One day these books shall be found in a tomb (post-apocalyptic Waterstones) and shall be the foundation of a new religion (hardcore cult). Side note: I am not being sponsored by Amy or Tina; however, I would be very interested in striking up a deal. Hit me up.

Amy and Tina speak at length about improvisation. In Queen Tina Fey's book she talks about the producers and directors of an improv-sketch company not wanting to make their company gender balanced because there weren't enough parts for women. And here I shall quoth our Royal Highness Tina Fey: 'We were making up the show ourselves. How could there not be enough parts?' Long story short: Dame Tina Fey got on that gender-balanced team without having to go all *Shakespeare in Love* on their asses. So there I am in my Yoda pyjamas thinking, *Hold up, Fey, I can create my own parts? I can be a doctor or lover or reindeer and not just an emotional tool or tick box?* Game changer.

So I signed up for my scary first improv class, and my world opened up.

When I'm improvising I am not limited by someone's expectations of me; I am propelled by the support of those around me. (That was some deep shizz. Please take a moment to recover before continuing.) Improv has allowed me to play the characters I've always wanted to play, which makes this sometimes restrictive industry easier to swallow. It's allowed me to play the whole of me and not just the fragments. I'm also fully psyched because I've got so much to learn about improv. Do you realize how awesome that is? People who want to become instant experts in a field they love are cray-cray. The joy is the learning, and the getting it wrong and doing it anyway.

In all my time improvising I have not once done a scene based around my disability. We've never ignored the fact that I'm in a wheelchair, and arguably all of my characters have been disabled, but it's never been the main focus of a scene. We've also never ignored the fact that I'm a woman but I have never been limited to the role of girlfriend or wife or secretary.

So, what do we do in a world in which the media representation of disabled folk is so minimal? How do we combat ableism when it comes to writing our stories and playing our heroes? Well, call me crazy, but we could stop having the discussion and actually get down to work. In the words of our Lord and Saviour Amy Poehler: 'The doing is the thing.'

I cannot speak for all disabled people. It's impossible. I don't understand what it is to be deaf. Or blind. I know what it's like to be a wheelchair user, but I would never say I could speak for all wheelchair users because that'd be verging on egomania. I also don't fully understand what it is to be a woman. I am one. I always have been, but I cannot speak for all women because again: cray-cray. I can however try to understand. I can educate myself. I can 'Yes, And' others.*

---

* 'Yes, And' is an improv term for accepting and building. It's about being open to new ideas and building on those new suggestions. Reader, I don't know who you are but as long as you are kind then I'm totally down for 'Yes, And-ing' you. I'd love it if you could 'Yes, And' me too.

A PLAYLIST FOR FEMINISTS IN ANY SITUATION

BY

COMEDIAN

It feels almost like a waste at this point to try to convince anyone to be a feminist. The internet is cheaper and faster than ever, and if there's ever a genuine curiosity about a group of people's experience, it's easy to research how they've been treated historically, and how social movements have improved their conditions. I'm not saying we shouldn't try, but I do feel you're either with us in this liberation movement, or the truth is you lack empathy for women, and you're just wasting our time.

So this is for the people who already identify as feminists: Hello! Welcome! Or, if you've been here for a minute, I hope you're comfortable. Allow me to set the mood with a playlist that will get you through some dark days and some big victories. (As of the writing of this essay, none of these artists were involved in a horrendous scandal that warrants throwing them and their music into a volcano.)

'You Oughta Know' by Alanis Morissette

This song isn't just a song; it's an anthem. For the scorned, the sexually liberated, the angry, the vindictive. Women deserve to feel and express all the emotions, and Alanis takes us on a roller-coaster of them. This song is best listened to before any march or protest to get you pumped up, after a less-than-ideal end to a relationship, or just screamed in joy at karaoke.

'Flawless' by Beyoncé

This song is even better as a music video remixed with Nicki Minaj, with the visuals and the lyrics displayed, big and bold and red, on that black LCD screen. In the original version we have Chimamanda Ngozi Adichie's words and voice loudly declaring, 'We teach women to shrink themselves, to make themselves smaller' and 'Feminist: a person who believes in the social, political and economic equality of the sexes'. It's so powerful, and then an actual angel, Beyoncé, reminds us that we woke up Flawless. An A+ song. This one is most enjoyable before a night out when you dance away all your worries. This is also just a celebratory jam for road trips to the grocery store or across your country.

'You Don't Own Me' by Lesley Gore

Maybe the original feminist anthem, this song is impossible not to love. Sweetie-pie vocals meet biting commentary about being your own free woman: few things are more powerful. Listen to this jam during any study cram sessions, sleepovers and general girls' nights out.

'Diamond Heart' by Lady Gaga

Perhaps you thought I'd say 'Bad Romance' for the Lady Gaga of it all because of the line 'I'm a free bitch, baby'. But no, in the vein of big, loud girl-fun, I have to go with the opening number from *Joanne*, 'Diamond Heart'. The story of a young woman dancing for money of her own volition, admitting she's not perfect but she's still got a diamond heart. That's a message I can get behind. Play this at your parties, and maybe also at your book club.

'I'm Coming Out' by Diana Ross

The world is going to accept you exactly as you are, and you're better than perfect, babe – you're *enough*. This is the perfect getting-ready song before any amount of fun is to be had. In the words of someone who didn't make this list, 'Your presence is a present.'

'King of Anything' by Sara Bareilles

This is that song for when you're hella fed up with somebody special's crap. Tell 'em what's what with this anthem that says, 'You're going to be half of this relationship or you're gonna be alone.'

'Just a Girl' by No Doubt

Is someone grating on your nerves? Do you need a sarcastic anthem to drown them out? Here it is. Imagine Gwen doing a ton of push-ups onstage in the 90s. Get your whole life.

'No Scrubs' by TLC

Women hold up the whole world. I truly believe that. They are the backbone of family structures, and are expected to put everyone else's existence before their own. Nah. Not any more. 'No Scrubs' is a song that will hold up forever, not only because of the iconic melody that's been used in Ed Sheeran's 'Shape of You', and is sung in bars and cars alike. It will hold up forever because it's unabashedly about reclaiming your time from scrubs who expect more than they deserve.

"WOMEN
HOLD
UP
THE
WHOLE
WORLD."

SUPPORTING
WOMEN

BY

ACTOR

Ten things I learned about what it means to support other women in a global community, following a trip to South Africa with the ONE Campaign:

1.

NO MATTER WHERE YOU'RE FROM OR THE LIFE YOU'VE LIVED, YOU'LL ALWAYS FIND SOMETHING IN COMMON AND A SHARED DREAM **WITH A FELLOW FEMALE**.

2. The education of girls is the most vital tool for development; they are the key to a prosperous future. Did you know that 130 million girls did not go to school today? ONE has a campaign called #PovertyIsSexist which calls upon world leaders to take action and make changes. There is nowhere on earth where women have the same opportunities as men, but the gender gap is wider for women living in poverty. Empowering women benefits their entire communities as they are able to give back.

3. Social media is a powerful platform for discovering and spreading a message. It sounds obvious, and I know the internet can be a scary place sometimes, but for so many of the girls I met, their time on the internet was their lifeline and their escape.

4. Listen more. Everyone has a story to tell or needs someone to talk to. You don't know what a difference you can make to someone's day by lending an ear. The ONE team inspired me to approach everything with an open mind, to check my privilege at the door and to listen, learn and share.

5. The trip was life-changing; I met so many incredible people and heard their stories. It's a privilege to be able to share this awareness. Knowledge really is power.

6. Positivity comes from community. Shared experiences keep people motivated and striving for more. The African proverb 'If you want to go fast go alone, if you want to go far go together' really resonates here.

7. The girls and women I met taught me to act on my values. Sometimes it can feel overwhelming to get involved, or like you won't be that impactful. But no matter how small the gesture, it is still powerful, and you are making a difference, particularly when women come together.

8. Autumn 2017, and the #MeToo movement was a harrowing indication of the prevalence of sexual assault and abuse. But this was just the tip of the iceberg of global gender inequality. If we care about sexism in our own countries, then we need to care about it everywhere. Hearing stories first hand was a shocking reminder of the scale of these issues.

9. Cherish the simple things in life. It sounds cheesy but it's true. Many of the girls I met found happiness in simple everyday activities and interactions. It could be watering a plant, or having a good chat. It reminded me to do more of this and not take it for granted.

10. We are incredible, capable, wonderful human beings. Let's celebrate, compliment and cheer each other on. Always.

GINGER

BY

Karen Gillan

ACTOR

When I was a wee girl, maybe around seven, I had bright orange hair, and limbs dangling off my torso like strings of spaghetti navigating a gust of unexpected wind. I was shy. The definition of introverted. An only child who preferred to exist in her imagination 'cause it was cool there. I was cool there.

There was one time I was walking towards my school. I had just parted ways with my mother and was making the leap from safety to the danger zone. It was waiting at the bottom of the hill. From afar I could already see two boys hanging around the entrance gate. I braced myself, took a large dry gulp and fixed my eyes firmly on the ground. Maybe they wouldn't notice me. Although that was a long shot when my hair was so bright I should have been giving out free sunglasses. And my skin was so pale any small amount of sunlight we saw in Scotland bounced off of me like a human whiteboard. Really the popular girls should have been friends with me. I would have reflected so much light on to them they would have looked even more flawless.

'GINGER!'

I kept my eyes on the floor. Maybe he meant someone else. We were in Scotland after all. There were tons of us.

'LANKY GINGER!'

OK, that did sound a touch more specific to me, but still, people are long in Scotland. Some people.

'TALL LANKY GINGER BITCH!'

There was no denial left. I stopped at the gate and slowly raised my eyes like they do in horror movies when they know the scary ghost thing is there and they have to look at it with all the dread in their being. I decided to say something.

'Lemmein.'

'WHAT?'

I cleared my throat. 'Let me in.'

'NUT.' Which is a Highland way of saying no.

The boys smiled because they weren't going to let me in and I wasn't going to do a damn thing about it. But then I remembered something and it brought the corners of my mouth up to match theirs. There I was, smiling back at them, which made their smirks contort with confusion. I remembered that my mother was still at the top of the hill, watching on, just waiting for a signal. I cranked my head round to see her poised.

'MAAAAM!'

And with that she came thundering down the hill. Her black hair sweeping dramatically to the side. Her strong limbs ready to take care of business. The boys quickly parted ways, opening up my path. I nodded to my mother who stopped halfway down the hill and watched me as I strode in, eyes fixed ahead, knowing one day I was going to be as strong as her.

"

I NODDED TO
MY MOTHER WHO
STOPPED HALFWAY
DOWN THE HILL AND
WATCHED ME AS I
STRODE IN, EYES FIXED
AHEAD, KNOWING ONE
DAY I WAS GOING TO BE
AS STRONG AS HER.

"

AN INTERVIEW WITH MY MUM

BY

ACTOR

MUM, AM I A FEMINIST?
ARE YOU A FEMINIST?
MUM, WHAT'S A FEMINIST?

It was the early 90s, and the word was new to me. It had been said angrily – sort of spat at me by some lad, when I'd argued about something. Apparently my short hair and unshaven armpits were all the proof he needed. I was twelve for fuck's sake, why would I shave?! At least let me get to my late teens before you completely annihilate my appearance. I could tell by the way he shouted,

'Shut up, you feminist!'

that he meant as an insult. It was, of course, a 'put down', a 'dirty word'.

I couldn't remember my mum's response. Surely she gave me pearls of wisdom for my amazing comeback . . . but, alas, I've forgotten the rest of this incident. So last night I interviewed her about feminism – phone recorder and all – while we waited for our takeaway. See, not all women cook!

Because today, 5 July 2018, at the age of thirty-six, sitting with my sixty-seven-year-old mother, I know the answers to these questions, but I'm curious. Was I brought up as one? Or did I become one? When did feminism become a part of my mum's world view? How as a parent do I, or we, instil a deep-rooted feminism in my daughter? When does the glass ceiling get shattered? How long has it been fucking up there?!

So the interview begins at 20:45 . . .

ME: So. Mum . . . actually, I'll call you Yvonne. So, Yvonne, when did feminism come into play for you? Do you remember?

MUM/YVONNE: I remember exactly, because I grew up in a village in Yorkshire in the 50s and knew nothing about it! Then my late teens and early twenties were the late 60s and early 70s, and women's lib was what it was all about. I was fully aware of it, and I thought I fully was it. I was single; I lived in London, away from home; I supported myself; I could get the pill.

ME: OK, OK, not so different – late teens for me were exactly the same . . . But I suppose the difference is, you hadn't felt any limitations or frustrations before that, whereas I was already angry by twenty.

I was angry that I was allowed to train with the youth

cricket team, but not allowed to be picked, as there were no girls allowed on the team.

I was angry that I got dragged out of a female changing room on a primary-school trip because they thought I was a boy. I had short hair for fuck's sake!

I was angry that drama school only accepted one third of women to two thirds men as there aren't enough jobs in the industry to justify training us all.

I was angry that my confidence to speak up would often be interpreted as bossy or 'she loves a little chat'.

I was angry that every time I threw a ball I was complimented by being told I threw like a boy. I don't throw like a boy; I throw like a girl who has been taught how to throw a ball. So fuck off.

Sorry, Mum, I think the takeaway is ready. Also, can you remind me to ask you more questions? I think I might be dominating the chat.

Interview suspended – 21:05.

22:30 – We've eaten; I've had half a bottle of wine; I'm ready to press record again.

22:35 – Interview resumed.

ME: Did you bring me and Kristian up intentionally gender-neutral?

The wine has confirmed that I am absolutely nailing this interview!

MUM/YVONNE: I don't think that term had been coined, but I wanted you both to have the same chances as each other and I wanted you to be able to be who you wanted to be. When I was growing up I wanted to be a teacher, but I was told by my parents that I wouldn't make it, so don't bother trying . . .

(This pisses me off so much; she would have been an amazing teacher.)

MUM/YVONNE: . . . I never wanted that for you and your brother, regardless of your sex. I just thought if I could make you confident and teach you that anything is possible, then I'd have done my job.

ME: OK, OK, that's brilliant. And thank you so very much!! I think that's maybe why I was so frustrated as a kid, because you guys never restricted us to gender roles, but you can't go anywhere without them being reinforced! I mean, watching some kids cartoons now makes me want to scream.

WHY HAS THAT CHARACTER BEEN DRAWN WITH MASCARA ON?
IT'S A FUCKING ANIMAL!

Why are those characters running and jumping, and that girl character is watching and giggling at the side?

Why, when I was at school, were no celebrated scientists, musicians, or playwrights women? Why are we only taught about the achievements of men?

Why, when women unite and come together with their voices raised, does the term 'witch hunt' get bandied around?

Why are some of my natural characteristics referred to as 'tomboy'?

I take a breath, and realize I've only asked her two questions and she already looks pretty tired! But I'm on a roll now – there's no way she's going to bed until we've smashed the fuck out of that glass ceiling!

ME: So, Mum, what do you want for women in the future?

MUM/YVONNE: I want my three granddaughters to be on a level playing field from day one. I want it to be illegal to discriminate, and legislation to be put in place that makes it pointless to discriminate. And don't just say wages are going to be equal – do it now. I want them to be treated with respect, and be equal without asking for it. I want things to move forward.

I press STOP.

One day my daughter might be interviewing me. Will it be the same conversation?

I fucking hope not.

"

I WANT IT
TO BE ILLEGAL
TO DISCRIMINATE,
AND LEGISLATION
TO BE PUT IN PLACE
THAT MAKES IT
**POINTLESS
TO DISCRIMINATE**.

"

FEMINIST COMEBACKS

BY

Scarlett Curtis

JOURNALIST, ACTIVIST

One of the first things that happens when you publicly declare yourself a feminist is that you start getting asked a lot of questions. As soon as you clip on the phone case or wear your T-shirt loud and proud, you are seemingly declaring yourself open for enquiries. If you're anything like me, these probes into your political beliefs will leave you a mumbling mess. I have read enough books and academic essays on feminism to fill a fairly substantial library, and yet as soon as I'm asked to sum it up I start sweating and string together a few unintelligible sentences before loudly shouting

'BECAUSE
BEYONCÉ'

and running to get another drink.

To save you from this embarrassing fate I have put together a collection of the feminist comebacks that I wish I'd thought of in the moment. Rip out this page, keep it in your back pocket and whip it out next time you're at a party or stuck in line for the loo with a drunk man at a party.

WHAT EVEN IS 'FEMINISM'?

Great question! It's actually something I'm really passionate about. Feminism is a centuries-old social movement fighting for the equality of the sexes. Intersectional feminists (I'm one of those) believe that all people are entitled to the same rights, and they fight to end all discrimination based on gender, sexual orientation, skin colour, ethnicity, religion, culture or lifestyle. I think bell hooks said it best when she said that 'feminism is a movement to end sexism, sexist exploitation, and oppression'.

WHERE I LIVE, WOMEN ARE ALLOWED TO VOTE AND DRIVE CARS AND RUN FOR PRIME MINISTER! WHY DO WE EVEN NEED FEMINISM?

Great question! Thanks for asking! You're incredibly lucky to live in a place where women have such a great quality of life but the sad fact is that those rights aren't universal. 50% of all sexual assaults worldwide are against girls aged fifteen or younger; one in seven girls in developing countries is married before the age of fifteen, and 131 million girls worldwide are out of school. In fact girls are 1.5 times more likely than boys to not attend primary school – that's 15 million girls of primary-school age who do not have the opportunity to access a basic education and to learn how to read and write, compared to about 10 million boys.

A feminist who only fights for the lives of women like herself isn't fighting for everyone, so I'm going to keep going at this feminist thing until *all* women have the same access to human rights. Also, in the UK, women earn 18.4% less than men do for the same work, and only 32% of MPs are women, so I wouldn't say our job is done here quite yet.

DON'T YOU WORRY THAT ALL THIS 'FEMINISM' IS GOING TO MAKE YOU REALLY UNATTRACTIVE TO MEN?

Great question! Glad you asked! The thing is, I'd rather not snog a boy who doesn't believe in women's rights or understand that the fight for women's equality benefits every human in the world, not just girls. Also, Margot Robbie's a feminist, and she seems to be doing just fine.

ALL THIS FEMINISM IS POLITICAL CORRECTNESS GONE MAD! CAN'T YOU TAKE A JOKE?

Great question! Thanks for checking! You're mistaken – I love jokes. I've actually got one for you . . .

Knock, knock!
Who's there?
Annie.
Annie who?
Annie thing you can do I can do for 18.4% less pay!

Ha, ha, ha. But, jokes aside, political correctness gets a bad rap, but all it really boils down to is minority groups asking that they not feel marginalized and hurt by everyday conversation or the media. I love comedy – in fact it is one of my favourite things. But I'm afraid that jokes that offend women, people of colour, disabled people, trans people, or others in the LGBTQ community just aren't funny to me. Let's chat when you come up with some better material, preferably something that doesn't offend my friends!

I'M A MAN AND SOMETIMES I FEEL LIKE ALL THIS FEMINISM IS MAN-HATING. CAN MEN BE FEMINISTS?

Great question! I'm so sorry that a misconception of the feminist movement in the mainstream media has led you to feel this way. Of course men can be feminists! In fact, the first British member of parliament to introduce a bill calling for women to receive the vote in 1866 was an amazing male feminist called John Stuart Mill. Daniel Radcliffe, John Legend and Prince Harry are also among the millions of brilliant male feminists, so you're joining a great gang.

The sad fact is that we've all been socialized from birth to accept sexism as a part of life and, as a result, women can actually be just as sexist as men. Institutionalized sexism (we like to call it 'the patriarchy') hurts men as well as women. It tells men that they aren't allowed to show emotions, that they have to be successful and powerful in order to succeed, and that they aren't allowed to like the colour pink!

Feminism is the fight to overcome all these things and also to ensure that women are given fundamental human rights like education, access to their own money and reproductive freedom. Feminists truly believe that if we lived in a world without gender-based oppression we'd *all* be so much happier – so, even if you're only joining for purely selfish reasons, we'd love to have you as a part of the gang!

DATA SOURCES:
www.globalpartnership.org/data-and-results/education-data
girlup.org/impact/why-girls

POETRY BREAK

PS don't worry – these poems are still totally feminist.

I DON'T FEEL LIKE A WOMAN

BY

Swati Sharma

ACTIVIST, POET

I don't feel like a woman.

I don't feel like a woman unless I look like a chandelier, which is to say I never do.

I don't feel like a woman unless a man looks at me, which is to say I rarely do but I do, the lechers on the streets make sure I do. Look at how they take away my identity only to give it back to me as something that makes my skin flinch, look at how I let them.

I don't feel like a woman when I walk into Sephora without knowing what, in fact, happens at Sephora. I don't feel like a woman, but I feel like a ghost, lurking upon some strange ancestral treasure I never really knew how to open or own.

I don't feel like a woman while I watch a James Bond film, or any film, which is to say I am used to it. I am the Mia Thermopolis who never finds out she is a princess because she isn't, who forgets she could've been a woman with or without the makeover, who wants the makeover but also detests the fact that she thinks she needs one.

I don't feel like a woman in a classroom or a business meeting, which is to say I am happy enough to be there. If joke could rhyme with woman, I'd put it in this poem, because I don't know what else I am when some unknown woman's assault becomes a punchline in the making.

Someday I might be a punchline too.

I don't feel like a woman because no man loves me, which is to say I have spent afternoons imagining hypothetical men singing my praises, each one of them telling me they love me for more than just my body but also my body, which is to say I don't.

I don't feel like a woman.

I feel like a token, an incident, some decadent creature sitting proudly upon its own ruins, which is to say by looking at me, you won't be able to tell that I don't feel like a woman.

Look at the way I fight with the marks on my face, how I fit in dresses that don't look like they're made for me, how I look at other bodies and suddenly find myself out of my own.

I don't feel like a woman but I am a woman.

Even after I cut my hair, refuse to wear make-up simply because I simply don't know how, which is to say when I do, maybe I will, but I spend every day convincing myself I don't have to, and when they say ask me, 'Are you even a girl?',

NO,

I AM A WOMAN,

AND I GET TO

DEFINE WHAT

THAT MEANS,

which is to say I will.

RECOVERING HYSTERICAL FEMALE

BY

Bronwen Brenner

POET

Powder-winged dovegirl

Frosted eyeshadow

Fallout pooling in your hollow collarbone

Is there such a thing as a right lavatory?

I'm a bitch, I piss on the daisies

I will one day push up instead of my tits

Slivers of ribs laid on silvery faux satin

Coquettishly feverish with my rouge blooming peony

Forsythia seeds bleed gold, behold Ariadne

Fill me with something I can be proud of for once

No more plastic jewels & mango Juuls

Lurid mercury signs flickering blue

Across vaselined eyelids

I want to be lucid and unobtrusive

No more swallowing nail varnish just to taste something

Garish glint of ultraviolet nativity scenes

Illuminating the lawns of parishes

Paring away at thighs with butterfly knives

Maraschino cherry juice squirting between teeth

My retainer smells like cunt and doesn't fit anymore

There has been a shift, a volta

Tectonic plates of my mouth shattered

Cobalt blue hued wedding china

Split down the middle

Scar your knees gathering fragments on the floor

I will pretend to be braiding your hair

As I trace the sutures of your skull

HE. THINKS.
I'M. AMAZING.

BY

Emily Odesser

POET

He. Thinks. I'm. Amazing. He.
Thinks. I'm. Amazing. He's
infatuated.
He's infatuated.
He can't stop his lolling head. He
can't stop his lolling head. He leaps
and stretches. He wants attention. He
wants me to notice
him like he's seen me do to others. He. Wants. My.
Energy. The spit that drips accidentally from my
pen in math class maybe. My attention. I do not
look his way. Boy
shocked. I don't know the color of his
eyes. I would not lift a finger if
a tiger was to bite him today. That boy wants
me. Does not know I harness all atomic
metals when my cells crash. Does not know I
sit on the sink and knead my shorts with soap,
knuckles melting
in the hot heat of water. Does not know this
is the beginning only. The boy
can jump to reach me all he wishes.
Why. Won't. I. Notice. Him. Poor
resigned boy.
He pleads.

Kid wants nothing more than to climb
deep into my head. Worm his way in.
Knock on the foamy muscles. Take
each finger and lull the thoughts towards him. This
boy wants to be a distraction.
oooOh he wants to pry me away. This
boy will get nothing.
Does not deserve me and you should follow
my lead and give him not a blink. He will take
the bat of an eyelash and run for weeks with it,
sort of elated. A kid this
crude, he knows this is the best entertainment he'll get.
So my craft is this. I do not blink when
he taunts me. I walk past his hard
stomach. My craft is this.
I do not dedicate this poem to him. My
craft is this. He thinks it torture. Hands
stone still,
eyes casual. He can't win me.

"

HE.

THINKS.

I'M.

AMAZING.

"

THE ~~FEMALE~~ WANK

BY

Grace Campbell

CO-FOUNDER OF THE PINK PROTEST

The first time I was turned on

I was eight.

Kim Kardashian's sex tape.

A girl in my class showed it to me after school.

My vagina felt like a hot air balloon.

I ran home so that I could finish the feeling alone.

I'll never forget it,

Sex with myself for the first time.

A feeling of utter bliss, and then suddenly—

I felt ashamed.

Disturbed.

Like I deserved to be locked up.

But I continued to do it. All the time, in secret.

A teddy bear. A pillow. A TV remote.

It was the biggest source of comfort,

And the biggest source of loneliness.

No one had ever told me girls could touch themselves.

Meanwhile, boys were being boys.

Wanking in the toilets at school.

Wanking alongside their friends to the same porn video.

A community of wankers.

Fathers were joking with their sons
about what type of porn they watched.
Cuming of age.

Boys were taught to think the female orgasm was as simple
as unlocking an iPhone.
All you need is a light fingerprint, and she will cum.
Sex with boys was a misunderstanding.
When it happened, there was no hot-air-balloon feeling.
He thought, *put it in there, and she'll enjoy it.*
Every time I so much as sighed, he thought it was an orgasm.
His pleasure was more important than mine –
My pleasure was locked up in the box of secrets.
I still thought I was a freak.
It wasn't until I was twenty that my friend told me
she did the same.
What I would have done to have known that
for all those past twelve years.
All that anguish wasted on nothing.
The next time I had sex,
I put my hand down there.
Showed him how it was done –
Whoever he was.

The sex I have with myself
Unlocks new levels of sex I have with other people,
Like *Candy Crush*.
Patriarchy has attempted to write female pleasure
out of our culture.
Patriarchy wants us to think our sexual gratification
can only be granted to us by a man.
But life is too short to be having bad sex.
Tell your mates –
Girls Wank Too.

SHARIA STATE (OF MIND)

BY

Emtithal Mahmoud

POET, ACTIVIST

I closed my eyes and waited for the men to leave, cold fear knotting my stomach as I lay on the floor, holding my younger sister close. I hoped for rescue, but the adults were all protesting in the town, well beyond our reach. At the time, my mother, sister and I were visiting our family in Darfur for the first time since we fled the government. That was eighteen years ago. It was my first glimpse of the type of conflict that would eventually become genocide in 2003. It's what inspired the poem 'People Like Us', and it's what had me standing in that same old house in front of different beds, packing a bag for a journey I had no idea how to prepare for. I was getting ready to walk 1,000 kilometres across Sudan in thirty days, and the people were already gathering in the square. My uncle, the same one who'd come home with clothes covered in blood from those he'd carried, either to safety or to rest, all those years ago, came intermittently into the room where my cousin and I were packing to check how much progress we'd made. 'You know you're going to be late? Why are you always late?' He's a lawyer, so he tends to get a bit nervous when things seem to be going wrong, but this time it was nervous excitement because he was beaming the whole time.

My uncle had accompanied me across Darfur as I conducted the first fully inclusive civilian peace talks in Sudan, hosting poetry town halls to get the ball rolling and collecting people's 'dreams for peace'. He asked me then the same question I knew he was about to ask me now as I threw my next pair of trousers into my backpack: 'You're going to wear trousers?' Everyone froze, from my cousin by the bed to our family members who kept piling their things into the room as well (we were busy organizing all the blankets together because we knew so many people would come).

'Khalu, it's literally a thousand kilometres,' I started, grabbing the next pair as he stared. 'I want to make sure I finish on time, not worry about hems and skirts and ridiculous rules.' My heart fluttered a bit at that point because I knew that being careful and clever with the rules had been the only way for us to create safe spaces for people to share their true feelings about peace in Sudan.

It is in little moments like these that I understand the importance and power that lies in our ability to remake a space. Since the war had taken so much from us, my great-aunt, the matriarch of that particular house, had decorated and redecorated the house innumerable times, growing gardens throughout my childhood to keep hope alive despite the sound of war planes and the uncertainty of leaving. Homemaking takes on a whole new meaning when home itself is burning. My aunts in turn stepped up their and their children's education, some going back to school after years of absence, some seeking jobs in the spaces they hoped would change the environment we lived in. Everyone in the family took their cue, working to keep their eyes on the future in the chaos that ensued. So there I was, following their lead – standing in the same house where I had hidden as a child, arguing with my uncle about the effect of my clothes on whether or not we'd be able to change the conversation around peace in Sudan.

It continues to baffle me that people's main concern about my activities around peace and grassroots activism in a full-on police state at first centred on my clothes – not my ideas, not my message, not my intentions; all those came second to what I was wearing and whether or not 'a girl' could walk that far. It made me think of women in power or actresses, musicians, even young women, how they are constantly performing on and off the stage; how so much of what people think of women is already decided before we even open our mouths.

'Seriously, we're about to change history and you're worried about my clothes!?' What's important to realize here is that I'm already a hijabi – I have been since I was eleven years old, when I took the decision myself. Now, for the first time, it felt like the decision was being taken away from me, like the part of my faith that I'd claimed as my own was falling into the hands of others.

I don't blame him, though, because my uncle's suggestions had come from experience – in the years since the war started many girls have been publicly beaten by law enforcement for wearing trousers. As a lawyer he's had to defend quite a few of them, and combats the worst in violence against women on a near-daily basis. Girls could even be arrested for indecency, a fact my aunt lightly reminded me of many months after the walk as I shadowed Noura Hussein's defence lawyers on the day of her appeal. My aunt's exact words – 'If you get arrested because of your clothes, you won't be able to help them get the death penalty revoked for Noura.' We did get Noura off death row, and it had little to do with what I was wearing – but that's another story for another day.

In the end I think change really does begin at home, at the dinner table, in a conversation, in split seconds, in quiet, determined moments. My clothing became just as big a demonstration as the walk or peace talks; my own existence became a protest too. This to me is the reason why feminism has to be championed on every front and in every space because, if we are not advocating for equality in every room, we may well lose this battle in the long run. Pushing back in public isn't enough, if we aren't all pushing back on the individual level each and every single day in person. And sometimes it's as simple as packing trousers.

THE VERDICT

In a gorgeous villa on the edge of Abu Dhabi
Fatima says to me –
It's like I'm either a whore or a saint –
is there no middle?!
An Arabic accent sanding the edges of her vowels soft,
her indignant question somehow capturing
the meaning of life in a few syllables,
my colourful scarf the inverse
of her black hijab,
and we laughed.
I want to tell her that I've felt the same every day
but never had anyone to ask this question
to. That we were standing in 'the middle'
outside the field of reason
and that some of us would die here.
Fatima's sister looked like a total vision
    in her hoop skirt,
a curly new haircut, her poetry notebook in one hand,
they called her the little rebel in the family.
Somewhere in Sudan, Noura Hussein was sitting
in a jail cell for killing
her rapist husband, an act of bravery
of self-defence of desperation.

People said – *What happened to Noura wasn't special,*
but her pushing back, that was different
as if she were rewriting history with her own
    shaking hands.
At home my mother would dress my baby sister
in what feels like a new country,
my other younger sister in a separate home
putting on her battle gear for work,
camera in hand, a selection of lenses in tow
ready to recast the world in her image.
I try to remind her that, no matter what they say,
the world really was made for us.
I meet with all these women in the span of a few months,
Noura's shackles jingling under her abaya
as she took a break from her studying
to meet my aunt and me, the warden looking
on with joy and hope at the community we found
in one another, her scarf set to match the army
green of her uniform.
There we were standing in 'the middle'
but, praise be,
none of us have ever died here.

" … IF WE ARE NOT ADVOCATING FOR **EQUALITY** IN EVERY ROOM, WE MAY WELL LOSE THIS BATTLE IN THE LONG RUN. **"**

ACTION

noun; *pronunciation* ˈæk.ʃᵊn

the process of doing something, especially when dealing with a problem or difficulty

things that are happening, especially exciting or important things

When a feminist 'gets some action', she does not in fact hook up with her crush but instead changes the world. Or does both.

FEMINISM IS A VERB, NOT A NOUN

BY

ACTIVIST, WRITER

In 1986 Marie Shear wrote in a review of *The Feminist Dictionary* that '[F]eminism is the radical notion that women are people.' A refreshingly simple definition, Shear's somewhat sarcastic assertion that the notion of women as people is 'radical' says a lot about the conditions experienced by women.

For me, Shear's definition captures perfectly the reason why feminism is a verb, not a noun. The 'radical notion that women are people' requires that one upholds the humanity of women at every opportunity.

In America, white women make 78 cents to every dollar that white men make. Black women make 64 cents to every dollar white men make, and Latinas make 58 cents to every dollar white men make.* Women are subject to daily harassment and threats of sexual violence, at work and in our communities. Our bodies are considered to exist for the sole enjoyment and discernment of men. Women are not seen as human beings, deserving of dignity and respect.

The socialization of the hatred of women is not solely perpetrated by men but infects women as well. No one experiences this more acutely than transgender women, who are shunned by cisgender men and women alike, often using the very same tropes that are weaponized by cisgender men to denigrate and oppress cisgender women.

The current US President, Donald Trump, made headlines for leading chants among his supporters during his campaign

* SOURCE: American Community Survey

to 'lock up' Democratic candidate Hillary Clinton, for paying off Stormy Daniels, an exotic dancer with whom he allegedly had an affair, and for being caught on video sharing his tips for assaulting women on the popular show *Inside Edition*, saying that all you had to do was 'grab 'em by the pussy'. You can tell that in America women are not considered people by many because, despite these examples of egregious behaviour, Donald Trump was still elected President.

Furthermore, the agenda of his administration works to strip women of the rights we've fought hard for – rights to have self-determination over our lives by deciding when and if to start families, and with whom, and rights to have access to affordable health care. The administration has led the charge to dismantle supports for families, such as TANF (Temporary Assistance for Needy Families) and SNAP (Supplemental Nutrition Assistance Program). In 2017, according to the US Census Bureau, 81.4% of single-parent families were headed by women, and a third of those families were headed by a woman who was unemployed. Cuts to government supports for families disproportionately impact women.

For me, this is why feminism must be a verb and not a noun. It is not enough to believe that women are people if our actions – for example, voting for a man who grabs women by the pussy and dismantles critical supports that enable women and their families to live with dignity – suggest otherwise.

TO WORK FOR A WORLD
WHERE WOMEN
ARE TREATED AS PEOPLE
IN EVERY ASPECT OF
OUR LIVES IS TO WORK
NOT JUST FOR WOMEN
BUT FOR ALL PEOPLE
TO REALIZE THEIR
FULL HUMANITY.

WOKE WOMAN

BY

Gemma Arterton

ACTOR

4:45 a.m. My alarm goes off. 'No Scrubs' by TLC.

Oh Jesus. Got to pick up James Bond from the airport. He's flying into Bolivia and has requested a British escort. I'm assuming an escort to the hotel . . . not the other kind. You never know with Bond.

I shower and dress in a hurry; it's going to be bloody hot and humid out there. Work prefer me to wear skirt and heels for occasions like this, but the truth is, I keep getting into scrapes with drug gangs, so that kind of attire doesn't cut the mustard – it makes it so much harder to run away – so flats and light trousers it is. And a modest blouse – I've heard about Bond's wandering eyes. I don't blow-dry my hair – it's only going to frizz up as soon as I go outside, plus I prefer the natural look. And don't have time for that stuff. Nor for a full face of make-up. Lip balm, sunscreen – that'll do – then I jump in the car, morning coffee in hand.

I meet Mr Bond at the baggage reclaim. He eyes me up, giving me the once over. I introduce myself. He makes some smarmy comment. 'Mr Bond,' I say, 'I'm not interested in flirting with you. I am here to work.'

'We'll see about that,' he says, sliding into the passenger seat of the car.

The journey to the hotel is spent trying not to feel completely put off by the fact that he's staring at me. He makes a comment about my driving. I talk of the week's agenda.

He's only half listening.

At the hotel, we check in. He makes some joke about us being teachers on sabbatical, which the concierge laughs at heartily. I've some forms he needs to sign and suggest we do them here, in the hotel reception. 'No, no,' he says breezily. 'Come up to my room. We can have a drink and it's more comfortable.'

'No thank you,' I say. Maybe he is attractive, but he's at least twenty years older than me, we've only just met, he's a work colleague – the list goes on. Plus this man has a reputation. Don't women who go up to his hotel room and sleep with him usually die in some horrific yet iconic way? No, no. Not me.

'Oh, come on, don't be so uptight. What's your name again?'

'Strawberry,' I say.

'Strawberry?! Oh yes, I've heard about you at MI5. Up for a promotion, aren't you? You don't forget a name like Strawberry. Do you know Penny Lane? Worked with her in Russia last year. I put in a good word for her, and look at her now.'

I know Penny Lane. Our parents all have a passion for The Beatles. Maybe she did get promoted, but she's also living with first-degree burns after an 'accident' in Moscow. Totally unrecognizable. Nearly died. Maybe *Mr Bond* didn't hear about that.

'No thank you, Mr Bond. If you could just sign these and leave them at reception. I have plans tonight. Have a pleasant evening.' I walk out . . . unharmed.

*

Driving through La Paz, back to my apartment, my car is, yet again, hijacked. It's a gang of three men. I take them down in an instant, thanks to my special-agent training. No weapons needed.

THANK GOD I WORE FLATS. ALTHOUGH A **STILETTO HEEL** MIGHT'VE COME IN HANDY . . .

Strawberry Fields is a fictional MI6 agent who features in the 2008 James Bond film *Quantum of Solace.* (*Quantum Of Solace* © 2008, Metro-Goldwyn-Mayer Studios Inc. and Danjaq, LLC. Directed by Marc Forster and written by Paul Haggis, Neal Purvis and Robert Wade. All rights reserved.)

STUFF YOUR POCKETS

BY

Beanie Feldstein

ACTOR

'What's the best piece of advice you've ever been given?'

Whenever I am asked this question, I instantly flash back to a very specific room: the Drama Lab. A cosy little room in the back corner of my high school where I rehearsed the countless school plays, musicals and improv shows I performed in during those important years. One of my most favourite rooms ever to exist.

While I learned several formative lessons in that room, the singular moment I always hark back to took place the day before I graduated high school. I was sitting on the floor in a circle with my improv troupe and our teacher, Michele. We were nearing the end of our final practice, a beautifully heartfelt farewell that left everyone extremely emotional.

I remember looking around at all the faces that I loved so deeply. The reality that this would be the last time we would all be together was starting to sit heavy on my heart. The anxiety of leaving high school began to rise to the surface, making my throat tighten.

Then I looked next to me at Michele as she prepared to give her concluding thoughts. This woman who had guided us through the intimidating world of improv, and also directed and choreographed the musicals that I cherished. A kooky, brilliant woman, bursting with passion and humour. She looked at us and stated simply: 'Stuff your pockets.' We all looked at her inquisitively. She declared again, 'Stuff your pockets.'

The words hung in the air around me as my throat loosened. I somehow knew exactly what she meant. It had absolutely nothing to do with collecting money or material goods. Instead, it was the notion of gaining understanding. Stuff your pockets. Learn from those around you. Hold on to everything and anything anyone is willing to teach you. Retain the knowledge the world has to offer.

Since then, I think about stuffing my pockets at least once a day. Sometimes once an hour, a minute. While Michele said it specifically in relation to performing, I quickly embedded it into every area of my life. To this day, it persistently fuels my curiosity. And I believe it to be the source of the little voice in the back of my head that told me to study sociology. I spent four years at university closely examining and critically analysing society. And while I always knew I believed in equality and the championing of women, by broadening my academic pursuits, I quickly realized just how much the patriarchy weighed heavy on every woman on the planet and how much that upset me. With each reading, each discussion with a professor or a classmate, the fuller my pockets became and the more feminism became a focus of mine. And the ideology of stuffing my pockets, or constantly seeking out the knowledge and experiences of those around me, became my personal approach to being a feminist.

Feminism is layered and its power comes from its diversity.

I am only one woman with one experience of the world. Therefore, alone I can only access a sliver of what feminism represents and holds up. However, when I actively stuff my pockets, I am filled with the brilliance of other women and their experiences. Therefore, I try to actively seek out the inspiring ideas, the maddening plights and important missions of other women. It makes my feminism more intersectional, more all-encompassing, more beautiful. Stuffing my pockets makes me feel powerful because it takes everything I already am but also adds the massive gifts of other women.

So, I try to constantly urge myself to never feel intellectually settled. That does not mean to say that I don't think I'm bright. Your old pal Bean knows she's a smart lady! However, I also know that there is always more to learn. I believe there are many ways to go about doing this. And I am still very much on my journey, so I do not claim to have the definitive way to go about this pursuit. That being said, there are a multitude of ways to stuff your pockets and most are quite simple and ridiculously enjoyable because there is nothing better than listening to the stories of remarkable women. I try to do this by reading novels, essays and articles, watching television and films, and listening to podcasts. And I'm sure I'm missing so many! But basically, if there is a woman with a story to share, I want to hear it. And then comes the crucial step involved in stuffing your pockets: to not only hear the story, but then take it in, fold it in to your own understanding and hold on to it forever.

My truest, deepest goal in life is to always feel constantly engaged with the humanity of other women. And, once again, I am just one woman with one experience of the world. So, in order to be the best feminist I can possibly be, I try to achieve my goal by consistently stuffing my pockets. Because we live in a world filled with ridiculously talented, smart, effervescent, powerful women, and I want to always have their brilliance with me. It makes me feel empowered to have their genius at my side whenever I need it. Whenever I feel lost or lonely, they are always right there, by my side.

So I urge you to try to always catch the beautifully varied female insights coming at you in this life and then hold them close. Take the wisdoms of the women in this world and keep them at your side. Always. As each woman commits herself to this pursuit, we grow as this pack of ultra-brilliant women, because we don't just carry our gifts, but the gifts of all women, as we continue on our journey to equality.

"

TAKE THE
WISDOMS OF
THE WOMEN
IN THIS WORLD
AND KEEP THEM
AT YOUR SIDE.
ALWAYS.

"

THE GLASS CEILING MUST FALL

BY

Lauren Woodhouse-Laskonis

GIRL UP TEEN ADVISOR (USA)

'If it's inaccessible to the poor, it's neither radical nor revolutionary' – Anonymous

Growing up in Rockford, Illinois, I was the younger of two children born to a single mother. In the summer of 2001, not only did my mom work full time as a nurse for the health department to provide for my sister and me, but she often had to sell things around the house when we were short on bills. Her hard work to keep us afloat ultimately couldn't sustain us, landing my family on WIC*. Now, as I'm leaving high school and about to enter the adult world, I realize how terrifying and daunting the responsibility of financially supporting two children all alone must have been. The worst part about this experience, however, is how common it is.

In the United States, 70% of the poor population are women and children. When we examine the major issues of today one may think of sexism, racism, homophobia or transphobia (all of which are inherently feminist issues). While attacking these issues are imperative in the fight against and the eventual fall of sexism in America, more often than not poor women and the various ways they are affected by these predatory issues are pushed aside in discussion even though women are the very people that make up these groups. For example, a fifth of transgender people have experienced homelessness at some time in their lives, and although African American women

---

*The Special Supplemental Nutrition Program for Women, Infants and Children, which provides food to supplement diets along with support and referrals to healthcare.

are the most educated population in America** poverty rates for African American women are the highest of any race at 28.6%. Moreover, due to the fact that only 19.8% of US congresspeople are female (but often well-off and white), poor women of every identity do not have proper representation in the very place that holds the ability to change how poverty is handled in this country.

When one sees how blatant a role poverty plays in the continued oppression of almost every population, including women, you have to wonder why this isn't a bigger talking point in feminist discussion. Whether this is due to the toxic narrative that poor people are poor by their own choice or the simple fact that women who subscribe to white, elitist feminism (as opposed to true intersectionality) forget poor and working-class women exist. The fact is, poverty is a feminist issue and it needs to start being treated as such.

As we further examine the interconnected web of oppression that deters virtually every woman from making their chip in the glass ceiling, the task may seem daunting. That's why when women from every identity support and listen to one another with the aim of understanding rather than pushing others' needs to the sides, we can all deliver the final hit needed to break the glass ceiling in order to achieve complete gender liberation. Don't sit on the sidelines. My mother and I will be there to watch it fall. Will you?

** Based on a 2016 survey by the National Center for Education Statistics.

"

WE CAN
ALL DELIVER
THE FINAL HIT
NEEDED TO BREAK
THE GLASS CEILING
IN ORDER TO
ACHIEVE COMPLETE
GENDER LIBERATION.

"

IF IN YOUR MIND YOU ARE BORN A GIRL

BY

Tasha Bishop

FOUNDER OF THE PANTS PROJECT

Not many women are told they were born without a womb. In fact, only one in five thousand of us are. From the day we emerge from our mother's womb, women carry the responsibility of one day holding another life in their own womb. We still live our lives according to the affirmation that women are mothers. Period (or, period-less). My sixteenth birthday present, along with a new pair of petal-pink Converse, was Mayer-Rokitansky-Küster-Hauser syndrome. I was told I had been born without a womb; I would never have a period, I would never give birth, and if I wanted to have sex I would have to undergo invasive long-term treatment. So, if I can't be a mother, if I can't contribute to the tampon tax fund and I can't be used for sex, how can I be a woman in this world?

I am so often asked why I started a charity selling underwear to raise awareness for women's issues and, a year on from launching, my reaction is still exactly the same. To cut a long story short, while I was in hospital having the treatment that would enable me to have sex, I struggled to define my identity as a woman, and felt particularly unworthy of feeling feminine in any capacity. My fairy godmother of a nurse advised me to buy some knickers that made me feel empowered – so I did, and it worked, and those pants are why I am here as a proudly unconventional, messy, multifunctional, mixed-up woman.

Despite being part of a mass movement some people are calling third- or fourth-wave feminism – a movement supported by millions of women and men all over the world – when it comes to telling my story, social anxiety still gets the better of me. I smile awkwardly, blush with embarrassment and wipe my sweaty palms down my jeans. I have created a community and project that I am incredibly proud of, built on women freely expressing and loving themselves, yet I am still soaked in shame when it comes to telling the story of how I went from an uninterested, grey-white granny-pants owner to an underwear enthusiast and 'Power Pants' advocate. I spend my days on the internet creating content to fight the patriarchy, promote feminism and empower women at all costs, so it is hard for me to admit that I still struggle with humiliation and a lack of confidence in being female . . . but I do. I am so aware and still hurt by the fact that I am not what society sees as a 'normal' woman, that my condition means I don't 'fit in' with society's standards of how a woman should be, and yet I preach day in, day out that we are all individually and beautifully unique, and should strive to embrace that, and be unapologetically ourselves. That's not to say I don't believe in my own manifesto, because I do wholeheartedly, but I am also human, and sometimes trying to be a positive, pioneering, patriarchy-fighting pinball of energy is challenging. We live in a world that is entirely visual, a world where seeing is believing, so, above all else, I do my very best to be honest. If the Pants Project does anything, I hope it reminds people of the beauty, truth, honesty and freedom in imperfection . . . because that is what pants did for me.

When women write about feminism, it can be destructive. We so often write about how our gender limits us, whereas perhaps a better approach is to think about what we can achieve in spite of the way society limits us through its construction of gender norms. This is the reason I started the Pants Project – to heal others, to empower others, to disable the stereotype of what it means to be a woman, but also to heal myself and remind myself of all the things I can achieve in spite of my limitations. On the days when it is hard to celebrate my arguably exquisite idiosyncrasies, I find myself writing for the Pants Project in a meditative way. By the time I reach the end of my post or piece, I remember the Pants Project exists to remind us that there is no such thing as 'normal', there is no defining factor of womanhood, and that being or becoming a woman doesn't happen overnight. No matter who you are, if in your mind you are born a girl, you will grow to be a woman through experience. It is not a biological process, it is not losing your virginity, it is not giving birth or raising children, nor is it a thing that can be calculated or defined: it is a staggeringly ineffable, gorgeous uphill battle from chaos towards a chosen selfhood of contentment, self-belief, self-love and empowerment. A battle that cannot be won unless women work together, build each other up and celebrate

" ... IF IN YOUR MIND YOU ARE BORN A GIRL, YOU WILL GROW TO BE A WOMAN THROUGH **EXPERIENCE**. "

each other's uniqueness. Women are not just mothers, we are multitudinous marvels, undefined by anything other than ourselves. Gender is a construct; but it is how we choose to move through our lives that makes us who we are. May the power of pants be with you.

PROVE THEM WRONG!

BY

Skai Jackson

ACTOR

Since I was very young I always knew I wanted to be an actress. Even when I was eight years old I would tell my friends in school how much I loved acting and modelling! A lot of people were happy for me, including my teachers and close friends, but some other people (mainly the boys) didn't show me much support. They would say, 'You really think you are going to make it big? You will never make it that far.'

It made me sad at times, but I was very determined and I knew I would fulfil my dreams one day. When we went to PE class, we would sometimes have to play basketball and the boys would say, 'Why do the girls get to play? Basketball is only for boys' or 'I doubt she will get a shot.'

Even though nothing they said was positive, it just made me even more determined to prove them wrong. If I had to give advice to my younger self, it would be: *Don't try to please everyone or prove yourself more than you have to*. I did that quite a bit in school, not realizing I didn't have to prove anything to anyone! As long as what I was doing made me happy, I shouldn't have to worry about anyone else's opinion. To me, being a girl is being independent, strong, empowering and caring, and supporting my fellow girls out there!

I AM PROUD TO BE AN INDEPENDENT, STRONG AND **EMPOWERING GIRL**!!

ON FEMINISM AND SHINING OUR LIGHT

BY

Maryam and Nivaal Rehman

GIRL UP CLUB LEADERS (CANADA)

Our names are Maryam and Nivaal Rehman. We are sixteen-year-old twin activists, journalists and high-school students currently based in Whitby, Canada. If the best moment in our lives could be described only using the colours that were most prominent, then we would say it was a moment of blue, black and white. There was something magical about the positive energy and happiness that danced in the air as little schoolgirls surrounded us in their uniforms and spoke about their dreams, as if nothing could get in their way. We were thirteen years old, visiting the Pakistani schoolgirls who had been a part of our lives for the past five years. To us, the girls represented the future. We always wanted to give them the opportunity to reach their truest potential, and had worked to convince the community to let them stay in school. The struggle in our village was a reflection of the problems that women and girls face around the world, as they lack many of the opportunities given to men and boys. However, when we support each other, those barriers can be broken, just as they were broken in our village. There, after years of workshops, conversations and convincing, the community finally decided to let the girls continue their education.

We still continue to work in our village, but at the time we realized that women and girls around the world need our help, and so we registered our Girl Up club. Girl Up's motto 'by girls for girls' is perfectly in line with our aim: to work for girls, locally and globally, through our own initiatives. Girl Up has connected us with a network of passionate, supportive girls, given us a platform to run our own initiatives, and has helped us grow tremendously as activists.

Feminism, which we define as the struggle to live in a world that gives equitable opportunities to all people, has been a vital part of our journey. To achieve the goals of feminism, we broke the norms in our society about a girl's abilities. Whether that was through taking leadership roles in our school for causes we cared about, taking risks when attending events as young journalists or sharing our story to inspire others, we did it all. We are nowhere near done, but progress has been made. Our message for girls and women around the globe is to shine. To stand up, take risks and chances. To find a tribe of unique, supportive women and girls who will lift you up, not put you down, and support them in return. Never be afraid of failure, but pursue your goals with the firm belief that you are capable of doing anything you set your mind to doing. After all, if we are to live in a truly equitable world, we women and girls need to work together, pursue our dreams and shine until our light cannot be ignored.

Luceat lux vestra
[let your light shine]

"

WE WOMEN
AND GIRLS NEED
TO WORK TOGETHER,
PURSUE OUR DREAMS
AND SHINE UNTIL
OUR LIGHT
CANNOT BE IGNORED.

"

BE A FUN FEMINIST

BY

Nimco Ali

ANTI-FGM ACTIVIST

Dear activist, sister and badass feminist,

As you read this you are either a full-on feminist or thinking about it. You might be starting a campaign, seeking to join one, or just pissed off at how fucked up the world is for women and girls. It's true, the patriarchy is fucking millions of us over and it seems like things can only get worse, but let me tell you a secret: things are changing, and we are winning. Women and girls across the world are standing together, speaking out and building movements that I believe will lead to a truly equal world.

These badass women and girls changing the world are just like you, so stop *thinking* about being a feminist and join us. There is no 'one size fits all' in the movement. All you need to do is care and want to change the world. If you do, you are a feminist and have been so forever. The day you were born a girl, even in one of the richest countries in the world, you were born to fight for everything you will have, want to have and do have. Ever since they blamed Eve for getting us all kicked out of the Garden of Eden, women and girls have been seen as something to fear and to be kept in their place. The tools the oppressor uses are different depending on when and where you were born, but at the heart of all of them is the ability to create fear. Fear of what might happen if you, as a girl or woman, step outside the narrative created for you.

Like I said, these tools come in different forms. I am going to tell you the story of how the patriarchy tried to break me and how, in fighting back, I found my feminist voice and today I am one in millions of women seeking to make this world better for generations to come.

Almost thirty years ago I was subjected to one of the worst forms of gender-based abuse. It was an act that was meant to break me, and it nearly did when I almost died at the age of eleven from complications due to FGM. FGM, which stands for female genital mutilation, is a procedure/act that involves the partial or total removal of the external female genitalia or other injury to the female genital organs for non-medical reasons. 'Non-medical' is the key word here. I was seven when I was subjected to FGM, and yes, it was painful, but it was also stupid, and that is what drove me to ask questions.

I was told that FGM was going to help me become a woman and in all fairness I think those around me believed that, but I did not. Until that moment, being a girl had been fun and not so different to what it was to be a boy. To be honest, I was not aware of the gender I was born into and how it had for centuries been the one under attack.

I was the only girl in the family, and growing up with brothers and uncles my age, we were all treated the same. We got the same access to school, love and toys, and everything was fine, but FGM changed all this for me, if not for those around me. As soon as I saw the woman who was going to cut me, I knew there was nothing good in her or what was about to happen. I had no context as to what was going to happen to me, but I knew it was not anything like the boys' circumcision. I had seen all the boys in my family taken to the hospital to be cut, and they came back limping, but there was never a sense of doom and gloom around them. The man who carried out the circumcision also did not look like death or a dementor (yup, those dark and evil things from Harry Potter).

Having worked in the fight against FGM, what I have found is that those who carry it out are sometimes as much of a victim as the child they are holding down. What they meant by telling me that I was 'now a woman' after my FGM was that the shock and horror of FGM should put me in my place. I was to keep silent. It was meant to instill fear in me; if this was how I was welcomed into womanhood, what else could happen if I did not play by the rules? Rules that included: 'girls should be seen and not heard', 'girls don't dream big' and for sure 'girls do not rule anything'. These rules, like FGM, are bullshit, and what I did not know is that my mother did not believe in them either. When I had FGM *she* was young and did not have the power to speak up, but what she did have was the power to raise me with the ability to not just rage but *roar*. So when I speak about the women fighting back, they are around us all, they are raising us, educating us, holding our hands without us knowing it. The moment I found out that my mum was a badass was the same day I officially became a feminist.

I remember it like it was yesterday. It was a spring day in March, and I was going to the doctor's for a check-up. A few months before I had life-saving surgery to undo some of the damage caused by my FGM. The relationship I had with my mum changed after my FGM. I was forever asking why, and getting nowhere so we kind of stopped talking and just became two ships in the night. As she was taking me to the doc's that day, a man came up to us. The man, who was some kind of distant uncle, spoke at my mum, ignoring me, and said, 'If you do not teach this girl how to dress, she will be lost to the whores of the West and become a feminist.' I was twelve, and I think that is the first time I really heard the word. I had no idea what a feminist really was, but what I did know and what I saw was my mother telling him that I was her daughter, and what I was going to be was great. Her words still ring in my ears, and as I stood there dressed like Scary Spice, I think I took on the power of my mum and the Spice Girls all at once.

I am going to let you into another secret: smashing the patriarchy can be fun. You can save the world, be a feminist and be cool AF.

The idea that my generation found their voice and feminism thanks to the Spice Girls is something that many mock, and others who think of themselves as radical feminists even find offensive, but it's true and I want you to know that you can find heroes and role models anywhere. When trauma or the patriarchy smack you in the face, what you need is some fun. For women and girls the world can be a dark place, and when you take on campaigning, that darkness can and will consume you if you don't look for some fun as you fight the good fight. So this is why I want to write this essay and share with you the reality: we are winning, and as we do it we are having fun.

The reason I love the Spice Girls is that they changed the world while never taking themselves seriously. They met world leaders and called them out on their bullshit. They sacked their manager and took on the music world and won. The Spice Girls were a revolution, and today when I meet prime ministers and presidents, I channel them as much as I channel my mum, grandmother and those who pushed a little harder every generation so I could stand as tall as I do today.

I hope as you read this you are singing a Spice Girls song. I hope you are planning your role in the movement, and I hope you are full of hope for a better world. If you still don't believe we are winning, let me tell you the final secret: on 11 October 2017 the number of uncut women and girls in my family outnumbered those who had been subjected to FGM.

FGM has been around for over four thousand years, and in less than eight years my family and many of those I know went from 100% uptake of FGM to zero in a generation. In my birth country and across the world FGM could end by 2030. I started my activism with a #MittsOffMyMuff banner. I took another seven-foot-long banner that read 'WE WOULD NOT CUT OFF YOUR DICK, SO DON'T CUT OUR CLIT' to the centre of London. This was not all for show, and this started a conversation. A conversation that led to the UK committing £36 million to ending FGM. The Prime Minister said that he was 'committed to ending FGM in a generation' as a result of me turning up at Number 10 dressed as a fanny.

Change is happening, and as I type this I am sitting next to my niece. She is seven months older than I was when I had FGM. She will never know FGM nor will her daughters or cousins. Sofia is a girl with dreams to be who and whatever she wants to be. And little girls with dreams become women with vision. Vision to shape the world as leaders and hopefully as fun feminists.

SO BE FREE, BE FIERCE, BUT MOST OF ALL **HAVE FUN** WHILE BEING A FEMINIST.

Oh yeah, and download *Spice World* – it is basically life.

THE POWER
OF THE PERIOD

BY

Amika George

ACTIVIST

THE PERIOD IS A BEAUTIFUL THING.

IT REMINDS US THAT OUR BODIES ARE UNIQUE, POWERFUL AND EXTRAORDINARY.

The ripening of an egg and the release of blood show that we have the ability to create and nurture new life. What could be more empowering than that?

I love that women everywhere (though not all menstruators are women), from the nomadic tribes at the foothills of the Himalayas to those women powering cities or multinational corporations, are connected and united by this wonderful, natural bodily process. Although most of us don't find ourselves marvelling at the mysticism of menstruation while straddling a hot-water bottle and cursing our balloon bellies, our periods are actually pretty incredible.

So, considering the sheer beauty of the period, why is there such a culture of shame and embarrassment surrounding menstruation? Why are periods so universally misrepresented and ubiquitously tabooed? Why do we euphemize and belittle them, stealthily hide tampons and pads up our sleeves, or skilfully manoeuvre, back to wall, when we anticipate the dreaded leak on to our clothes? The reason is simple: misogyny.

The period is, and will always be, an issue that is exclusive to women. The one thing that women have and men don't. But, because periods don't affect men and we live in a deeply patriarchal world, they are shrouded in shame and apology. Put simply, if men had periods, bleeding would be an Olympic sport and there would be free menstrual cups given out on the Tube.

The period is undoubtedly a feminist issue. The Tampon Tax only reinforces this: given that Jaffa Cakes, bingo games and vodka jellies are deemed essential, tax-free items and menstrual products are not, women are being taxed for simply being women. It's symptomatic of society's view of women, whose needs can be readily overlooked. The tax reeks of injustice and misogyny in every sense, and only accentuates the presence of the patriarchy and our need for feminism today.

Growing up in a family of strong, empowered women, and going to a girls' school in which we were taught to discard any implication that gender would ever hold us back, I always viewed feminism as an important part of my life. My great-grandma will always be my ultimate feminist hero. She was born in the 1920s in South India, and refused to live her life within the boundaries set out for her. She had an arranged marriage, but in her thirties, at a time when women were not expected to accomplish much more than marrying and starting a family, she left behind her two young children and flew to the USA alone to start a Masters in Journalism. She did exceptionally well, and made lifelong friends in Ohio, before returning to India and becoming one of the country's top journalists, writing about women's issues. She continued to defy expectations, retiring as a university professor, and didn't stop writing, learning and asking questions until she died last year, at the age of ninety-two. She taught me the importance of embracing the unknown, and refusing to confine yourself to what others deem right or conventional.

Feminism today is changing. In the past, women like my great-grandma were certainly feminists, but often they didn't know it, or at least they didn't call it that. Now, though, the term is more used and embraced than ever before, and I think social media is responsible for that.

It's incredible that, as the term has grown more 'mainstream', it's become cooler, more accessible and more inclusive than ever before. From slogan T-shirts to Instagram bios, feminism is everywhere, and it's so amazing to see teenage girls, particularly, so empowered. I'm so excited to watch the next generation of teenage feminists make their

"

FROM SLOGAN T-SHIRTS
TO INSTAGRAM BIOS,
FEMINISM IS EVERYWHERE,
AND IT'S SO AMAZING
TO SEE TEENAGE GIRLS,
PARTICULARLY, SO EMPOWERED.

"

mark on the world because I truly believe they're going to achieve extraordinary things.

Starting #FreePeriods, the campaign to end period poverty in the UK, showed me just how powerful passionate teenagers can be, collectively. Last year, after reading an article that stated that children in the UK were routinely missing school, often for one week every month, because they couldn't afford to buy menstrual products, I started an online petition calling on the government to provide free menstrual products to those already receiving free school meals. These were the children from the lowest socio-economic backgrounds, who were struggling to afford even the most basic, inexpensive pads and tampons. Some resorted to making their own makeshift alternatives using socks, toilet roll or newspaper.

I couldn't believe that there was such abject poverty in the UK, and I was horrified that our government hadn't acted to eradicate period poverty immediately. It's clear that the disengagement and subsequent lack of attainment that comes when girls miss large chunks of the curriculum create a marked gender divide in educational progression, leaving these girls trapped in the clutches of poverty and deprivation.

Very quickly the campaign grew, and teenagers everywhere were calling for an end to period poverty, and for these girls to be given back their education and their dignity. Even today,

I am overwhelmed by the sense of solidarity and community that #FreePeriods has formed and nurtured. Our protest outside Downing Street in December 2017 saw two thousand young people, dressed from top to toe in red and waving banners emblazoned with period puns, come together to call for an end to this injustice, and, more widely, to celebrate the period. In March the government allocated £1.5 million from the Tampon Tax Fund to help charities end period poverty in the UK – a fantastic progression on the path to ending period poverty, though we are still calling for a long-term statutory pledge to ensure that every child is going to school. If we want to stop periods from inhibiting educational progress, negatively impacting girls and thus obstructing our fight for gender equality, there's still a lot of work to be done.

Right before our eyes, the world is changing radically: societal taboos are being smashed, we tolerate more, dictate less, and embrace change like never before. Finally we're shouting about the silence. And, unsurprisingly, it's young people who are driving the force for change. As the #FreePeriods protest demonstrated perfectly, young people are completely unrivalled in their determination, passion and willingness to bleed for their cause.

Before we begin to dismantle the archaic and oppressive taboo around periods, we need to ensure that EVERY child in this country is getting the education they need and deserve. If a period is holding them back, we have a serious problem on our hands and the government needs to step in.

So, Theresa May, if you're reading this, watch out for the rise of the bleeding teenager. We're armed with jumbo tampons and we're ready for the fight.

FEMINISM ONLINE

BY

Whitney Wolfe Herd

ENTREPRENEUR, FOUNDER OF BUMBLE

I didn't mean to become the poster girl for online harassment. Believe me, I wouldn't wish that on anyone! I was twenty-four years old and I'd left my first job in a very public way. (That's a story for another time.) As too many women have learned, the internet can be a terrifying place if you find yourself in the headlines, especially if it's anything to do with gender.

I was ripped apart by strangers: rape threats, death threats, the works. The misogynistic abuse I experienced was so painful. I felt as if it had started to define me, like a scarlet letter. The way shame, guilt and blame attach themselves to women, even when we aren't at fault, is so dangerous and pervasive.

I let myself wallow a little. For months I suffered anxiety attacks. I drank a lot of wine. But I couldn't let hate bury me. I wanted to find a solution, and to help others in my position. Really, if I'm honest, I wanted to build a feminist internet. All the social platforms and online networks out there were created and/or run by men. What would they look like if they were taken apart and created from scratch with a woman at the helm?

As I was being bombarded by hate, I kept my head down. I was hard at work on a prototype for a women-only social network. I was going to call it Merci, and it would be a way to spread compliments. I thought I'd combat the harassment I had experienced with love and kindness. I thought there was room for an online platform where positive behaviour was contagious. But my now-business-partner Andrey had another idea. He knew that my forte was the online dating space.

At the same time I was watching as my girlfriends – brilliant, independent women – waited. They waited for a guy to ask them out. Waited to be texted back, or to receive a message on a dating app. Waited for 'the one' to come along. And I watched them being branded 'clingy' or 'crazy' for refusing to play that game. It had always bothered me, but now I felt a renewed sense of urgency.

For all the advances women had made in the workplace and corridors of power, the gender dynamics of dating and romance still seemed so outdated. I thought, what if I could flip that on its head? What if women made the first move, and sent the first message?

If I couldn't fix the internet, I could at least launch a dating platform where misogyny and all its attendant shame, guilt and blame had no place.

In the four years since, Bumble has grown beyond a dating app into a fully fledged social network, where women make the first move in all parts of their lives, from romance to making new friends and professional connections.

We're the first platform of our kind to ban misogynistic behaviour. We don't allow disrespect or hate, whether that manifests itself in sexist language or an unsolicited dick pic (yeah, they're the worst!). We're rewriting the antiquated rules of society that we want to see reflected in the real world.

When we're labelled a 'feminist' app, I feel a pang of pride. It means women don't just have a seat at the table – we're building a whole new table, and adding seats to it. And that scarlet letter has become a badge of courage. It reminds me that I refused to be defined by the worst thing that ever happened to me.

WE DON'T HAVE TO LET NEGATIVE EXPERIENCES BURY US; WE CAN USE OUR PASTS **TO FUEL US**, **TO DRIVE CHANGE**.

That's become a very real part of my feminism. We see those years of negative treatment by men, by institutions, by the patriarchy, by society at large. We see it. We challenge it, we stand up to it, and we change it.

A FEMINIST CALL TO ACTION

BY

Jordan Hewson

ACTIVIST, TECH ENTREPRENEUR,
FOUNDER OF SPEAKABLE

It wasn't until I got into the workplace that I realized gender equality was not a given; it was something to claim. The older I get the more I discover the depths, the more I realize sexism is a carefully architected *system* that might take longer than we think to truly decode; that fact alone makes me aware that I am, at twenty-nine, still a feminist with training wheels.

My feminist triggering started at twenty-three. This is likely because, up until that point, I had been in college, where girls could perform as well as or better than boys, and therefore the idea that boys were entitled to more or better things didn't just seem ridiculous, it seemed uneconomical (which it is), and since everyone kept talking about suffragettes and Second Wave Feminism (apparently Third Wave Feminism didn't make it to Irish schools in the 90s), I assumed that feminism was more a fact than it would be a future.

It was that same year I read an article about a fourteen-year-old girl being shot by the Taliban for advocating for her own right to go to school. This was Malala. Reading her story on the *Guardian* website, I was entirely outraged but I never once questioned what I could do, and as I got busy I forgot about the story and continued my day answering emails.

About an hour later, I caught myself and started to wonder: if I cared so much, why wasn't I doing anything?

Fast-forward three years. I launched a software product called Action Button. Our goal is to close the gap between inspiration and action by connecting people to solutions in real time so they can take action in the moments that matter. My journey as a founder of a tech company has been challenging, given my only formal qualification is a master's degree in poetry (try explaining that to venture capitalists – or anyone really). I started to discount myself, doubting whether I could pull this off, but I soldiered on with the initial help of YouTube tutorials: 'What is Excel?' and other topics for poets starting companies. Truthfully, I had no idea what I was in for and the odds are still against us, but I'm proud of our mission: to build a product that can integrate social action into our daily lives, mostly in response to news stories, so we can make a positive difference to those stories and an impact bigger than a hashtag every single day. Basically, we're trying to put the 'like' button out of business.

So how do we, as furious feminists, take action to advance opportunities for women? Here are two ideas.

1. MAKE SEXISM SEEN

Sexism is a context through which we can understand our world, and the economic, social and political structures that govern it. Sexism is a culture. Yet somehow I often feel as though we're at war in the dark; sexism must become visible. I believe that is our first weapon as feminists: identifying sexism, and helping others see it too. Sexism isn't always obvious; in fact most often it's contested. If you witnessed the 2016 US election, you'll know how many people disagree on where, when and how sexism manifests. Let's be honest, you probably have people in your own family who fight with you on the topic over dinner. You might yourself have unknowingly propagated a sexist attitude because of social influences – I certainly have made that mistake. Whether we're male or female, we need the tools to identify sexism. I am persistently surprised by not only the extremity but also by the subtlety of the patriarchy. Let's not underestimate it.

Just look at some of the ways in which sexism is cultured. This will anger you:

Sexual harassment
'Slut'-shaming
Economic inequality
Gender wage gap
Workplace inequality
Lack of education access
Lack of sexual and reproductive health
Objectification
Domestic abuse
Lawful marital rape
Body shaming
Unpaid care and domestic work

" SEXISM MUST BECOME VISIBLE. I BELIEVE THAT IS OUR FIRST WEAPON AS FEMINISTS: IDENTIFYING SEXISM, AND HELPING OTHERS SEE IT TOO. **"**

Lack of political representation

'Likeability'

Lack of leadership positions and equal opportunity

Luxury taxes on feminine products – 'the pink tax'

Child marriage

Female genital mutilation

Sexual slavery and prostitution

Maternal mortality

Rape and sexual violence

Gender selection

Discrimination against mothers

The list continues. A host of awful experiences with one causal source: the oppression of the female sex. How do we tackle something so insidious, contested and, at times, invisible?

I do not have the answers but my second question is: what on earth do we do?

2. REACT INTO ACTION

If you're reading this book, I'm so glad, for many reasons, but mostly because you are also searching for answers and your ideas will be better than mine. Your actions might start with giving your dad (and maybe your mum too) a feminist reading curriculum, or petitioning your university to include feminist texts in Philosophy and Civics (or pretty much any) courses. I can only speak from my own experiences. Starting my company was not a logical decision since I really didn't know where to begin. But I did it in reaction to a story of a girl who had been braver than I could dream. Her story made me brave; I believe we're here to do that for each other.

Sexism expresses itself in multiple forms as a chameleon to power. You might think you're tackling one form of it as you discover the next. Malala's story is about being threatened out of a classroom and it led me down the path of venture capital, where I was confronted with an entirely different type of discrimination I hadn't anticipated. In the United States last year, female founders got only 2% of venture capital funding, proving there is work to be done in every industry.

Although the source of the discrimination we face is the same – the fact of our gender – the expression and effects of that discrimination can vary wildly, often based on where you live. There are female voices out there carrying testimony you might not relate to, but they can provide you with a source of hope or fury that will translate into only one thing: energy. Use it.

"

THERE ARE FEMALE VOICES
OUT THERE CARRYING
TESTIMONY YOU MIGHT
NOT RELATE TO,
BUT THEY CAN PROVIDE
YOU WITH A SOURCE
OF HOPE OR FURY
THAT WILL TRANSLATE
INTO ONLY ONE THING:
ENERGY. USE IT.

"

CO-PARENTING

BY

Sharmadean Reid

ENTREPRENEUR

For me, supporting lone parents is a starting point for equality. It's the foundation that allows other conversations to happen, like increasing the economy and productivity of a nation and improving its Gross Domestic Happiness.

Most of these lone parents are women.

For the women who choose to start a family, they cannot even begin to think about taking incremental steps in their career if they are unable to work because of the domestic and emotional labour they have to endure, unpaid.

Of course, we should be supporting families whatever they look like, but ultimately there is a difference between single (lone) parents and co-parents.

Co-parenting can happen whether you are still with your partner or not, and whatever your sexual orientation. Co-parenting can happen without a partner at all. For those who have moved to a new city and don't have their biological family around to share the child rearing, a strong network of 'aunties' or 'uncles' is invaluable.

We made co-parenting the norm in our household before my partner and I separated and we still work that way. We have a 50/50 split, half the week at my place, half the week at his. This is uncommon but incredibly important. Why?

- I would not be able to run my business without my son's father to share half the childcare load.

- My business currently employs twenty other women. I've been able to create work opportunities for others because of my domestic set-up.

- But, most importantly, and this one is a little more esoteric, I would not have the headspace to come up with innovative ideas and take my business to a global level if my mind was occupied by all the small daily tasks women have to handle in the home. This is a luxury.

Imagine if every woman had this advantage – how many new businesses would spring up? How many more unbiased technological innovations would we have? How many more women would have great jobs as a result? I am working towards this in two ways:

- I'm helping girls to start applying critical thinking to their position in life very early by supporting an organization called Fearless Futures. As they get to school-leaver age, this critical thinking will enable them to *write their own rules* on how they should behave at home and at work. Like asking for co-parenting at home or for more money at work.

- I ensure that my business gives shared parental leave, so that men have the opportunity to take on domestic roles too.

After that, all the other work can focus on improving the situation for women in the workplace. *We just have to get them there first.*

Who wrote the rule that single fathers only see their children every other weekend? This was a plot line that I scrubbed out of my life. I am not going to pretend it was easy. I would budget five years of emotional hardship for you to hold on to consistency and routine, and to discover with your co-parent what works for you both and your child together as a family. It's not an easy ride, but stand firm! I promise, it's worth it.

Encourage the women around you to challenge societal norms and write their own rules on the balance between work and home. Promote positive images of involved fathers, empowered, not emasculated.

I BELIEVE THAT UNLESS WE CREATE GENDER EQUALITY IN THE HOME, WE CAN'T CREATE IT AT WORK.
THESE SMALL CHANGES WILL GET BIG RESULTS.

DISMANTLING AND DESTROYING INTERNALIZED MISOGYNY: TO-DO LIST

BY

WRITER

- Remember that when you stand in front of the mirror and examine the depth and width of the lines on your forehead (every morning) and feel a throttling rise of panic, it's probably not because you're some really deep thinker with a profound sense of the passage of time and a complex relationship to death that no one understands. Instead, it is simply years and years of conditioning from magazines and films and TV telling you that a woman's worth diminishes with age. This is bullshit constructed by men who are trying to make you hate yourself, spend masses of money and waste every waking moment thinking about how to avoid a fundamental inevitability of life. Ignore it.

- Remember that when you stand in front of the mirror naked and examine every opalescent stretchmark and knobbly toe and undulation of flesh of your body (every night) and feel a deep, sour hum of self-hatred, it's probably not because you're hideous. Instead, it is simply years and years of conditioning from magazines and films and TV telling you that there is only one specific type of body shape and skin colour and nose and toe and hip and waist and cup and arse size that is acceptable. This is bullshit constructed by men who are trying to make you hate yourself, spend masses of money and waste every waking moment thinking about how to change everything about yourself. Ignore it.

- Don't judge women on how they choose to parent. It's hard enough already.

- Don't use the language of your oppressors – it's unhelpful and it's lazy. That means difficult women aren't 'bitches', sexually free women aren't 'sluts', expressive women aren't 'mental' and passionate women aren't 'psycho'. Also – always argue that 'cunt' can't be the worst word in the world because it describes one of the best things in the world.

- While ingesting culture steeped in very traditional gender politics, don't feel guilty about it, but have your patriarchy ultrasound switched on at all times. Enjoy romantic comedies while knowing that it will take much more than a man to bring you your happy ending; watch *Gone with the Wind* and acknowledge that your fetishization of toxic masculinity probably came from watching Rhett Butler and his moustache and all that shove-y snogging when you were thirteen and it was the only thing on TV on Boxing Day.

- If you have a problem with the way a woman is 'doing' feminism, don't call her out on it publicly or humiliate her in front of your peers. Write her an email or, even better, take her out for a glass of wine, some debate-y gesticulation and robust barking.

- Remember that when a woman gets the job you wanted or dates that bloke you fancied or wears a dress you loved but couldn't afford, she hasn't taken anything from you. There is time and space for you to do it too. One of the cleverest things the patriarchy did was make us believe that there is only one tiny sliver of success cake available; that we all have to fight over it; that a woman who tramples on all her competitors to chow it down first is somehow 'ruthless' or, to borrow a phrase from *Apprentice*-ese, 'a natural business mind'. This is a scaremongering lie. There are so many cakes to eat. And if you can't find the slice you want, try baking one. Cake for everyone! Let them eat cake! I've got lost in the metaphor.

- Addendum to previous point: actively help other women find their slice of success cake, irrespective of whether you've got your slice yet. Celebrate those who've found their cake – stick candles on top and sing them 'Happy Birthday'. I've overstretched the metaphor again, haven't I?

- When a woman is acting like a bit of a shit, take a moment to recall the tiring, embarrassing, humiliating, oppressing, frightening, demanding, overwhelming, totally unfair bollocks you've had to put up with since you were born on account of your gender, and question whether this might be at the root of her difficult or defensive behaviour.

- Also accept that sometimes women are just a bit rubbish, and that's OK too. But really exhaust the previous point first.

- Don't judge other women's looks – or compassionately but firmly check yourself every time you do. Show women the courtesy you wish society would show you. Don't competitively look at other women's bodies in the gym, don't define a woman by her appearance, don't sit around looking through Facebook photos of your boyfriend's ex-girlfriend with your friends, saying things like: 'I suppose she's pretty, but in a very boohoo.com way.'

- Don't say that all you want is for women to know their value and be unapologetic about their achievements and take up space and present with confidence, then, on meeting a woman who is doing just that, think to yourself: *She's a bit full of herself, isn't she?*

- Don't trivialize something as enormous as how to fix a toxic culture that makes women turn hate in on themselves and then out on each other with some natty little millennial listicle.

- Be patient with yourself, be patient with other women. Be OK with getting it wrong. Have the humility to recognize your mistakes. Don't self-flagellate. Acknowledge that the patriarchy is a cult that so many of us have been enrolled in without our consent and that de-programming may take a while.

REMEMBER THAT THE JOURNEY WILL BE WORTH IT –

AND THE LESSONS WILL BE GREAT ONES.

PERIODS

BY

Adwoa Aboah

FOUNDER OF GURLS TALK, ACTIVIST, SUPERMODEL

Who remembers their first period? Or has had to check their seat before standing up? Or, my personal favourite, has experienced the panic of realizing you've bled all over someone else's bed? OK, now who's on their period today? Ironically, mine literally came on last night.

As the founder of Gurls Talk, I'm determined to end period poverty. Our periods are still being taken for granted and undermined, and this is a feminist issue. That there is a *luxury* tax on sanitary products, items so necessary in our day-to-day lives, shows you how unimportant the government deems menstrual hygiene and women's health. And this simply isn't good enough. We should not be taxed for a totally normal bodily function. We need to be talking about this. Tell your mum, confide in a friend, share on your socials, lobby your local MP and talk to your teachers.

This is not just a women's problem. We need men's help. Talk to your dad, break the awkward silence with a brother, make sure that they know about the difficulties women face when unable to access sanitary products, and the wider impact this has on society. We demand to be heard, and won't be ignored. Girls, smash the taboo and talk.

Through constant conversation and discussion, we can normalize periods for those who still insist on making them abnormal. Let's recognize what must be done to help women around the world and ensure they are given the necessary menstrual provisions. Fuck yeah!

EDUCATION

noun; *pronunciation* ˌedʒ.uˈkeɪ.ʃᵊn

the process of teaching and learning, or the organizations such as schools where this process happens

If you weren't born with a natural understanding of the meaning of the patriarchy, we would like to inform you that you are not alone and invite you to check out your local library and see if they have anything written by bell hooks.

BAKER-MILLER PINK

BY

Scarlett Curtis

JOURNALIST, ACTIVIST

WHAT IS THE PATRIARCHY AND WHAT CAN THE COLOUR PINK DO TO STOP IT?

In 1985, Dr Alexander Schauss, Director of Life Sciences at the American Institute for Biosocial Research in Tacoma, Washington, began a study on the psychological and physiological responses to the colour pink.

In 1969 Schauss had become intrigued with the effects of colour on the human brain. Schauss's experiments found signs of relaxation in subjects when they stared at a cardboard plate of a certain shade of pink. Their heart rate, pulse and respiration were all lowered and such a response was not observed in reaction to any other colours. Schauss began to think that perhaps pink could have an effect on human aggression, so began to formulate the perfect shade. After experimenting with hundreds of colours, Schauss found a mix that had the maximal effect on reducing hostility – P-618, RGB code: 255, 145, 175.

In 1979 Schuass began to take his experiment to American prisons. He convinced the directors of a naval correctional institute in Seattle, Washington, to paint some prison cells pink so he could measure the results. The rates of assault before and after the interiors were painted pink were monitored and the navy's report stated: 'Since the initiation of this procedure on 1 March 1979, there have been no incidents of erratic or hostile behaviour.'

IT WAS FOUND THAT **JUST TEN MINUTES IN THE PINK ROOM** WAS ENOUGH TO DRAMATICALLY REDUCE VERBAL AND PHYSICAL AGGRESSION AND CALM A PERSON DOWN FROM A PLACE OF EXTREME VOLATILITY.

Schauss named the colour Baker-Miller Pink and went on to perform numerous studies across the globe, which all reported that this particularly shade of pink led to dramatic reductions in aggressive behaviour.

While there is no conclusive evidence to show that Baker-Miller Pink genuinely changes the human brain, we are using it on the cover of this book, in combination with the book's contents, to enact a little experiment of our own on a certain form of human aggression that we like to call 'the patriarchy'.

Patriarchy is a word that gets thrown around a lot and, for those of us who aren't feminist scholars, the word can sometimes be hard to properly define. The dictionary definition of patriarchy is 'a system of society or government in which men hold the power and women are largely excluded from it'. This means that whether you're a man or a woman, even if you have the best intentions in the world and believe that all men and women should be equal, you're still participating in a global society in which women are disadvantaged. It's a bit like joining a club whose mission is to put straight white men in power and oppress minorities, and even if you don't take part in their activities you're still a part of the club. The only problem is that the club is the whole world and we're all members.

The patriarchy has hundreds of little boxes and it doesn't like anyone stepping out of them. It demands that those in power promote aggressive and hostile behaviour, and that those who don't have power never break through a double-glazed, impossible-to-penetrate glass ceiling. The patriarchy is everyone's enemy, whether you're a man or a woman, because it reduces human freedom to a set of prescribed rules and demonizes those who try to break the boundaries.

The patriarchy means that women are under-represented in key institutions and industries; it leads to male violence against women and it enforces standards of behaviour, meaning that women feel they need to be beautiful and weak, and men feel that they can't show emotion. This can result in toxic masculinity, which teaches young men to hide all emotions except anger.

The patriarchy reinforces gender stereotypes. The goal of the feminist movement is to combat this. It aims to give each person on this planet the freedom to live their life the way they want to live it, unhindered by sexism or oppression or aggression. The goal of the feminist movement to remove these hostilities is not that far from the goal of the scientist who invented Baker-Miller Pink.

DATA SOURCE:

Schauss, Alexander. (1985). The Physiological Effect of Color on the Suppression of Human Aggression: Research on Baker-Miller Pink. *International Journal of Biosocial Research*. 7. 55-64.

"

THE GOAL OF THE
FEMINIST MOVEMENT . . .

AIMS TO GIVE EACH
PERSON ON THIS
PLANET THE FREEDOM
TO LIVE THEIR LIFE
THE WAY THEY
WANT TO LIVE IT,
UNHINDERED BY
SEXISM OR OPPRESSION
OR AGGRESSION.

"

IF YOU CAN'T SEE IT, HOW CAN YOU BE IT?

BY

FOUNDER OF HERSTORY UK

THE URGENT, NECESSARY, HUMMING CENTRE OF MY FEMINISM IS **SHARING WOMEN'S HISTORY**.

Four years ago I was floored listening to a radio programme on women's history, and for the first time realized my life was only possible because of the radical actions of women generations before me. I felt more present just for knowing that they had lived. I felt bigger, taller, fuller – like I could take up more space in the world. The impact was real, physical and, for me, life changing.

I soon felt angry at how the education system had let me down. By the time I left school I was used to donning a beard. I wore one with a tea towel as a shepherd in the Nativity play, another for World Book Day when I came as Shakespeare. My most inventive beard was when I swooped my hair in a ponytail beneath my chin to take on the persona of William the Conqueror – with a moustache that, frustratingly, was of a different shade. In all this time, I had never seen a boy in my class dress up as a woman unless it was for a joke. On Red Nose Day a boy arriving in a tutu would induce peals of laughter; on the last day of term we would squeal with hilarity when a male teacher wore a dress and heels. Is the idea of being a woman really that side-splittingly funny?

I thought about the times in school I'd been asked to take on the role of a historical man and done so happily. I wondered which women from history the boys in my class could celebrate with me. I looked for them in maths and found only Pythagoras; I thought about my English classes and saw Shakespeare. I cast my mind back to science lessons and remembered Watson and Crick. Where were the women in my education? I did some research and found out they were there, women were everywhere, in the same subjects I had been taught – except I hadn't been told about them. I was learning <u>His</u>tory but never <u>Her</u>story. I felt that girls everywhere were being denied their right to envisage themselves in what they were learning and consider the variety of futures that could spool out ahead of them.

I'm often asked why I think women's history isn't shared more widely. My answer has been simple: the patriarchy. However, it's more than that – it's about what we are looking for when we seek to gain an understanding of the past. Recently, I was commissioned to do a piece of research about women working together, and it blew my mind. Behind most major changes that affected the lives of women worldwide, there is a whole host of women who made it happen. I realized that women's history is in the most part not about one person; women have worked together to make change and yet the way we share stories is so often about an individual. We hang our past on figureheads.

WOMEN'S HISTORY IS **BIGGER THAN ONE PERSON**, SO THE WAY WE TALK ABOUT THE PAST NEEDS TO BE AS WELL.

Collective working is often dismissed as idealistic and impractical, but my research showed me the opposite. The first rent restriction laws came into being because of the Glasgow Women's Housing Association, who looked out for each other. When the bailiffs came to unfairly evict tenants someone would sound the alarm and all would flock to the house, throwing flour bombs and causing chaos, forcing the bailiffs to retreat. It was the Hackney Flashers, a community of London mums, who through their exhibition 'Who's Holding the Baby?' got the first state-funded childcare centre opened. In Botswana, the Emang Basadi Women's Association had the Citizenship Act amended, so Botswanan women could keep their citizenship if they married a non-Botswanan. The Ford sewing machinists brought about the Equal Pay Act. The list goes on and on. Women working together have achieved tangible life-changing results and should not be underestimated.

I am delighted to share with you five groups of women who have supported each other, pooled their resources, stood in sisterly solidarity; women who have created change and found joy, purpose and meaning in doing it together.

CHUPIREN

In 1970s Japan the women's group Chupiren were also known by their other name, which translates as 'committee to stop women from crying themselves to sleep at night'. They would come together and share personal stories of their day-to-day lives. When women shared that their husbands were abusing them, the group would unite and go together to his place of work. They wore pink helmets emblazoned with the symbol of the woman and marched into offices unfurling large flags, chanting, 'We will not accept the tyranny of the husband.' If the husband himself was not at work, they would knock on the door of the boss and challenge him, arguing that he should not employ someone who abused their partner. At this time in Japan both domestic violence and divorce were taboo subjects; Chupiren sliced directly through what was considered acceptable to win justice for each other.

THE FEMINIST PARTY

Formed by lawyer Flo Kennedy, the Feminist Party was determined to change the face of American politics forever. Flo and the other members knew that feminism was inherently political and shouldn't be locked within academia. Over forty years before Barack and Hilary battled it out, the Feminist Party created a platform for Shirley Chisholm to run for the Democratic presidential nomination. She was the first woman to run for nomination and the first African American person to do so as part of a major party. This group of women were strategic; they suspected that Shirley might not win, because they were told countless times that America would not accept a president of Shirley's race or gender. Shining the spotlight on such a compelling candidate showed the world that although America may not have been *ready* for Shirley, Shirley sure was *ready* for America, so America had better catch up. Shirley said: 'If they don't give you a seat at the table, bring a folding chair.'

ANTI-MISS WORLD PROTESTORS

'We are not beautiful, we are not ugly – we are *angry*' is the chant that rang around a surprised auditorium at the 1970 Miss World beauty pageant in London. As over 24 million people tuned in to the most-watched TV programme of the year, it was the Women's Liberation Movement that stole the show. The presenter Bob Hope was presenting the bikini round when a claxon sounded and the protestors, dotted around the auditorium, erupted from their seats, throwing flour bombs and tomatoes, causing complete chaos, dashing along the aisles as they were pursued by security. As the world came together to judge the beauty of women, these protestors came together to abolish women being judged in this way. They did not seek to shame the models but rather dismantle the structures that established women as decoration to be pitted against each other and critiqued by men; in their own words, they wanted to 'ban this cattle market'.

STAR

Best friends Marsha P. Johnson and Sylvia Rivera were pivotal to the gay rights movement in America as organizers, activists and advocates. The pair had been celebrating Marsha's birthday at the Stonewall Inn when it was raided by police. Marsha and Sylvia were among those who instigated the Stonewall uprising against the police, now synonymous with the beginning of the gay rights movement. The movement would go on to systematically exclude them. Both Marsha and Sylvia knew from experience that it is trans women, particularly trans women of colour, who experience the sharpest edge of patriarchy and who are most at risk. When attending gay-rights meetings they realized that trans youth were not being properly represented or considered by the organizations they were involved in. Together, they founded and paid for STAR, the first activist organization to support trans young people living on the streets. They advocated on behalf of and forged a safe space for trans people, often teenagers who had been kicked out of their homes and were living on the streets of New York.

THE BODYGUARD

In 1913 the Cat and Mouse Act was introduced, where suffragettes who went on hunger strike in prison were released just long enough to get their strength back before being arrested again. In response, a group of women formed the Bodyguard, to protect those the police were keen to arrest. This courageous group came together in secret locations across London to train in the martial art jiu-jitsu, determined to become a physical match for the police. As well as being skilled in martial arts, each woman hid a wooden club up her skirt for good measure. At demonstrations they would take on the police personally, delaying them from accessing the main speakers at events, ensuring there was maximum time to rally the crowds before the event got shut down. The Bodyguard embodied the suffragette motto 'Deeds not Words'.

I hope these stories sit with you a while after reading this chapter. Maybe the flags of Chupiren will unfurl in your mind as you walk into an office, or the chant of the Anti-Miss World Protestors will ring in your head the next time you feel underestimated. I hope you will share these herstories with others, that you'll look up the individuals involved and the causes they fought for. I hope you can make space in your life for them, so that together we can poke holes in the canon that encases us all, holes that many more herstorical women can clamber out of.

FOR ME,
PRACTISING
WOMEN'S HISTORY
IS A POLITICAL ACT;
BE DELIBERATE
WITH YOUR SHARING,
STRETCH THE STORY OUT,
MAKE IT BIG ENOUGH
FOR ALL OF US TO SEE
OURSELVES IN.

For further reading visit herstoryuk.org or follow @herstory_uk

A SHORT HISTORY OF FEMINIST THEORY

BY

Claire Horn

ACADEMIC, WRITER

INTRODUCTION

Feminist theory might seem daunting at first. For one thing, it can seem like everyone already has more context than you – and it can be hard to know what to ask or where to start. Even the idea of 'theory' can be off-putting: how do we disentangle that word from visions of dry academic debate happening behind closed doors?

But here's the exciting thing about feminist theory: unlike many fields, feminist scholarship has always been deeply tied to women's experiences. This work has always been interdisciplinary, informed by developments in pop culture, and defined by knowledge built from the challenges of everyday life.

It's true that there's a lot to read out there, and it's also true that there are many contentions and contradictions within feminism. Today, the more frequently used term is 'feminism[s]', recognizing the fact that, while there are many shared goals, there are also divergent concerns, aims, strategies and practices within the movement.

This timeline is designed to give you a quick overview; just like feminism itself, it cannot possibly be contained in such a small space. But this is a starting point, from which you can get an idea of where to go to explore many different schools of thought, contradictions and debates.

The history of feminist thinking is often described as

occurring in three (or four!) waves. In reality, these categories are more messy and overlapping than this, but it's a good place to start!

FIRST WAVE (MID 1800s–1920s)

The beginning of the 'first wave' does not necessarily mean the beginning of the feminist movement. In fact there were plenty of women, both individually and in groups, who identified the rights of women as an important cause well before then. Just one example of an earlier feminist text is Mary Wollstonecraft's *A Vindication of the Rights of Women*, published in 1792 and well worth a read for the contrast with how we articulate our feminist causes today (for instance, Mary insisted that women were fundamentally more gentle than men). However, the beginning of the first wave in the mid 1800s is largely seen as the point at which a movement dedicated to securing fundamental rights for women – the right to vote, the right to own property, the right to education – began to take hold as a mainstream cause.

1848–1860s

The 'birthplace' of the first wave of feminism is often traced to the American Seneca Falls Convention in 1848. This meeting, convened by Elizabeth Cady Stanton and Lucretia Mott, took the civil liberty of women as its subject. Many of the women who would become central in the push to secure voting rights attended, and a 'Declaration of Sentiments' was read, which included this twist on the Declaration of Independence:

'WE HOLD THESE TRUTHS TO BE SELF-EVIDENT: THAT ALL MEN **AND WOMEN ARE CREATED EQUAL.**'

Many of the feminists who initiated the first wave had begun as activists organizing for the abolition of slavery. In fact some of the leaders were inspired to begin a women's movement by their experiences of being denied the opportunity to speak publicly against slavery alongside men. The attendees at the Seneca Falls Convention included Frederick Douglass, the orator and writer who was born into slavery and initially fought for universal rights for black men and for women.

You may have noticed that none of this sounds like 'theory'! But in fact that's where it all begins. The texts and speeches that circulated at this time are early documentation of the ideas, desires and activism that shaped this field. In Ohio in **1851**, Sojourner Truth (Isabella Baumfree), also born into slavery, delivered what would become known as the 'Ain't I a Woman?' speech. In response to a man describing what he argued were fundamental differences between men and women, Truth said, 'That man over there says that women need to be helped into carriages, and lifted over ditches, and to have the best place everywhere. Nobody ever helps me into carriages, or over mud-puddles, or gives me any best place! And ain't I a woman?' If women were so delicate and feeble-minded that they shouldn't be allowed to vote, why were black women enslaved and abused? Truth pointed out a fundamental contradiction here, and, like other women of colour who supported the feminist cause, she emphasized the importance of thinking about race in this movement. Truth's speech – and the work of other black activists like Anna Julia Cooper and Hallie Quinn Brown, who insisted on the liberation of black people and women – informed later feminist theorists. Unfortunately, in the 1860s rifts formed between the mainstream feminist movement and the movement for racial emancipation.

1860s–1890s

In spite of the continued possibility of the shared goal of universal human rights, following the American Civil War and the abolition of slavery a division emerged between suffragists like Elizabeth Cady Stanton and Susan B. Anthony (who felt that women's voting rights must take priority) and activists including Frederick Douglass, who emphasized emancipation for black men. In 1868 the Fourteenth Amendment granted citizenship recognition to all American men, and in 1870 the Fifteenth Amendment extended the right to vote to include black men. At this time some suffragists, including Lucy Stone and Julia Ward Howe, continued to organize to identify shared causes. But it is important to look back on these moments in the history of feminism. Some of the strategies used by leading white feminists at this time, including Stanton and Anthony, involved explicit racism and exclusion. In the emphasis on women's rights to the detriment of the rights of black people, women of colour were sidelined in this early movement, in spite of the fact that many of these women, including Sojourner Truth and Ida B. Wells, fought for both causes. In 1890 the National American Woman Suffrage Association was formed, and began pushing for voting rights on a state-by-state basis, and in 1896 the National Association of Colored Women, including leaders like Anna Julia Cooper, formed to support the inclusion of women of colour.

In the United Kingdom the tide turned in the 1860s, with suffragists gathering and agitating for basic rights, identifying the injustice of the continued denial of the vote to women. The first big attempt to secure women this right was presented in parliament in 1866 by John Stuart Mill. Its rejection only fuelled the fire, leading to the formation of women's liberation groups in cities across Britain. It's important to remember that there were rifts here, too. In the late 1880s many men living in poverty did not have the right to vote either, and while a number of the leading groups campaigning for suffrage had working-class women among their members, the mainstream movement was led by middle- and upper-class women who often did not consider the interests of poor and working women. In 1897 the National Union of Women's Suffrage was formed, led by Millicent Fawcett, which pursued votes for women using non-violent means.

1900s–1920s

Another important contingent emerged when, in the early 1900s, Emmeline Pankhurst became the leader of the Women's Social and Political Union. Though initially the group had included working-class women, in 1907 a number of these left the WSPU, feeling that it was too focused on the concerns of 'ladies'. Some later joined other contingents such as the East London Suffragists and the Women's Freedom League, which explicitly used pacifist strategies to further their cause.

Though these groups all pushed for suffrage, their strategies diverged. Where the Fawcett-led branch and the Women's Freedom League were suffragists who campaigned using rhetoric as their key tool, the WSPU, composed of suffragettes, engaged in tactics from hunger strikes to storming parliament to window smashing. They were also met with violence: on 18 November **1910**, later known as Black Friday, women who marched to parliament to protest the rejection of a bill to grant votes to women were brutally attacked.

In spite of the fact that the stakes for many working-class women were extremely high – they had to balance long working hours and childcare with organizing, as well as suffer more brutal treatment when they were arrested for their activities – a number of them, including Selina Martin and Dora Thewlis, were key to pushing the movement forward. Additionally, though suffragism in the UK is often regarded as a predominantly white women's movement, women of colour, including Bhikaiji Cama and Sophia Duleep Singh, who also fought for Indian independence, were central to the cause.

FEBRUARY 1918

One hundred years ago, the Representation of the People Act passed in the UK, and extended voting rights to all men, including working-class men, and to women who owned property. In 1928 the Equal Franchise Act passed and granted all women the right to vote.

AUGUST 1920

Through efforts at national organizing, the Nineteenth Amendment was introduced in the United States at the federal level, granting women the right to vote. Until the Voting Rights Act passed in the 1960s, however, discrimination and violence against people of colour attempting to vote continued to occur at state level.

This is in *no way* a full history of the first wave of the women's movement, but it's a snapshot to get you reading! So, we know that the first wave took voting rights for women as a key cause, but it was also motivated by equal rights to education, and full property and financial emancipation for women. It was significant, too, for the emergence of contentions between the causes of black liberation and the women's vote, between working-class movements and rights for middle- and upper-class women, and between more radical strategies and pacifist ones. All these tensions are a part of the history of feminist theory, and they deeply inform later work. Though we will leap ahead to the second wave, there were of course key moments in feminism between these 'waves'.

FEMINISM DOES NOT **HIBERNATE**.

SECOND WAVE (1960s–EARLY 1980s)

If the first wave began with a focus on achieving the right to vote, the second wave was all about full equality: equal rights in the workforce, sexual liberation (and access to contraception and abortion) and freedom from intimidation and violence. The 1960s and 70s were also the era in which feminist theory as we know it today was born, and it saw the beginning of women's studies as a discipline.

1949: Oops! This doesn't look like it belongs here, and this speaks to the slipperiness of the 'waves' as categories for feminist theory. French philosopher Simone De Beauvoir wrote *The Second Sex* in 1949, in which she critiqued the workings of patriarchy and the historical and continuing degradation of women. The English-language version of the book, published four years later, grew in popularity in the United States and Britain during the early 1960s, and helped to shape the goals of the movement.

1960s–1970s

1963: Betty Friedan's *The Feminine Mystique* took up the feeling of malaise and disenfranchisement among American women homemakers. Friedan argued that American housewives, and particularly women who had worked outside the home during the war, were suffering from the 'problem that has no name', a deep and abiding unhappiness

"

IF THE FIRST WAVE BEGAN WITH A FOCUS ON ACHIEVING THE RIGHT TO VOTE, THE SECOND WAVE WAS ALL ABOUT **FULL EQUALITY** . . .

"

that underpinned their seemingly idyllic lives. bell hooks, among other black feminist and womanist writers, would later critique the exclusive focus of Friedan's work on white middle- and upper-class women, noting that, while Friedan suggested that a key problem for women in general was wanting a career beyond their homes, for many black women, other concerns, such as poverty and the necessity of pursuing often difficult work, were more pressing. In addition, hooks would note that the movement of white women outside their homes often meant that women of colour would need to take on this labour instead. However, Friedan's work, along with De Beauvoir's, became central to building the mainstream second-wave feminist movement.

Also in **1963** journalist Gloria Steinem disguised herself as a Playboy Bunny, and reported on the sexism and harassment she experienced and the racism she witnessed while undercover. Steinem, who continued to campaign around sexual harassment, abortion rights and women's equality in general, would go on in the early 1970s to found the feminist magazine *Ms.*, together with feminist activist and racial justice organizer Dorothy Pitman Hughes. Pitman Hughes was a leader in establishing women's shelters in New York City, and the two toured together and spoke on race, class and gender justice.

In **1966** the National Organization of Women (NOW)

formed in the United States; it was committed to action for equal pay for equal work, sufficient childcare support, the ratification of the Equal Rights Amendment to include full protection for women, and the availability of safe contraception and abortion. In the UK, women organized around similar issues, with the Dagenham women's strike at Ford in 1968 helping to kick off a movement towards equal pay and fuller work opportunities for women.

1967 saw the decriminalization of abortion in parts of the UK (England, Scotland and Wales), though it remains illegal in Northern Ireland.

In **1970** UK feminist Sheila Rowbotham called a Women's Liberation Movement conference in Oxford, which was attended by many of the women who would go on to write key texts in feminist theory, and at which participants discussed key demands for the movement, including equal pay, the availability of daycare centres, and full access to contraception and abortion. In 1971 the first National Women's Liberation March occurred in London, and in the early 1970s Reclaim the Night marches, dedicated to ending violence and sexual abuse of women, took place throughout the US and UK.

In **1973**, with the Supreme Court's Roe v. Wade decision, abortion rights were granted to American women. Also in 1973 Margaret Sloan-Hunter founded the National Black Feminist Organization, and later the Women's Foundation.

Literature throughout this era corresponded with and addressed this liberal, rights-based movement. In particular, the late 1960s and early 1970s saw a surge in writing from radical feminists. In the UK, in **1970** Kate Millett penned *Sexual Politics*, in which she argued that patriarchy shaped and limited women in every aspect of their lives. *Red Rag* magazine, published by a Marxist contingent of the Women's Liberation Movement, addressed many of these issues as well. In the United States Carol Hanisch, Shulamith Firestone and other members of radical collectives, including the Redstockings, New York Radical Women and New York Radical Feminists, held speak-outs at which women shared experiences of sexual violence, harassment and abortion, and insisted that the 'personal [is] political'. In **1970** Robin Morgan, a member of NY Radical Women, edited the first edition of *Sisterhood Is Powerful*, another key text in second-wave feminist theory, which included work from black feminist civil rights lawyer and advocate Florynce Kennedy, and Frances M. Beal, who founded the Third World Women's Alliance.

LATE 1970s–1980s

As in the first wave, women of colour noted the ways in which the mainstream feminist movement often failed to address their concerns. The Combahee River Collective, a black lesbian feminist organization, convened numerous times between the late 1970s and early 80s. In **1977** the group released a statement from founding members Demita Frazier, Beverly Smith and Barbara Smith, in which the authors stated their shared goals of challenging sexual, racial and class oppression, and outlined the struggles of women of colour against sexism in the black liberation movement and racism in the mainstream feminist movement. The group is often credited with coining 'identity politics', a focus on the ways in which different aspects of identity shape one's experiences. Barbara Smith continued to play a key role in black feminist scholarship and activism, beginning the Kitchen Table, a publishing press for women of colour in **1980**.

In **1981** *This Bridge Called My Back*, co-edited by Gloria Anzaldúa and Cherríe Moraga, brought together work that considered 'the complex confluence of identities – race, class, gender, and sexuality – systemic to women of color oppression and liberation' as a key site of enquiry. In **1987** Gloria Anzaldúa's *Borderlands: The New Mestiza*, in which she unpacked her experiences as a Chicana feminist and lesbian woman, also became a key text in feminist theory.

In **1983** author and activist Alice Walker defined the term 'womanist', writing in her collection *In Search of Our Mothers' Gardens: Womanist Prose* that 'Womanist is to feminist as purple is to lavender.' Womanism, for Walker and many black women who have followed, was a way of distinguishing the ways in which the voices, goals and needs of women of colour feminism were distinct from the movement that had been dominated by white women. Other important black feminist thinkers, including Audre Lorde, Angela Davis and bell hooks, have written and spoken on the importance of feminist praxis that acknowledges the specific ways in which race, class, gender, sexuality and other aspects of people's identities shape their experiences. Also published in **1983**, Gayatri Spivak's *Can the Subaltern Speak?* critiqued a tendency within second-wave feminism to reduce women outside the Western world to objects in need of rescue. In the UK, the *Feminist Review* released a special edition on Black Feminist Perspectives in **1984**, including an essay from Valerie Amos and Pratibha Parmar called 'Challenging Imperial Feminism', in which these authors, too, shared this concern about the tendencies of the mainstream movement to treat women outside the West as unable to speak for themselves, and about the limits of the movement in addressing the concerns of black British women. In **1988** *Charting the Journey: Writings by Black and Third World Women*, edited by Shabnam Grewal, Jackie Kay, Liliane Landor, Gail Lewis and Pratibha Parmar, further explored and engaged these issues.

The second wave then focused on matters like equal pay for equal work, freedom from sexual and physical violence, and access to contraception, childcare and abortion. It also saw the birth of feminist theory as we know it, arising from feminist publications and the emergence of newly instated women's studies programmes. Just as with the first wave, contentions emerged, radical strains diverged from more liberal mainstream ones, and women of colour pointed to the ways in which racial and classed identities were central to the forward movement of the cause.

THE THIRD WAVE (1990s–2012)

During the third wave, feminism expanded, transformed and, following on from the limitations of the second wave, became many movements. A number of things happened that kicked this wave off. In 1991 law professor Anita Hill accused Supreme Court justice Clarence Thomas of sexual harassment. Both Hill and Thomas were African American, and many felt that the subsequent dismissal of Hill's accusations reflected a failure to trust the testimony of black women and to recognize the important links between racial and gendered oppression. Rebecca Walker, daughter of Alice Walker, wrote a response piece to the event for *Ms.*, in which she heralded the arrival of feminism's next wave, writing, 'I am not a postfeminist, I am the Third Wave.'

"

'I AM NOT
A POSTFEMINIST,
I AM
THE THIRD WAVE.'

"

The third wave was characterized by many causes, including campaigning for and the successful passage of the 1994 Violence Against Women Act in the United States. During this time, punk rock riot grrrls were also hitting the scene, demanding to be heard, and, in academia, women's studies was beginning to morph, shifting from feminist theory focused solely on women to considering gender more broadly. In 1990 the beginning of queer theory in academic feminism had a radical impact outside the university.

Again, there is a slippage here between waves, because, if we've learned anything about feminism, categories can never fully contain it! Along with the texts by feminist scholars of colour that were released in the late 1980s, there are a number of other theoretical texts that became key for feminism's third wave.

Between the late 1980s and the early 1990s authors including Eve Kosofsky Sedgwick, Judith Butler and Gayle Rubin emphasized the importance of thinking about the distinction between 'sex', the biological identity assigned at birth, and 'gender', the aspect of identity which, these scholars argued, was socially constructed. The idea that the extent to which a person was 'male' or 'female', and whether or not they identified with either of those categories at all was not predetermined but malleable, would become a key aspect of feminisms to come. Queer theory, of which these authors and others are considered to be founders, has influenced the way in which we think about sex, gender and sexuality, and has importantly emphasized that inclusive feminism needs to consider these parts of our identities.

In 1989 American law professor Kimberlé Crenshaw coined the term 'intersectionality'. Crenshaw described different aspects of a person's identity as being like intersections in a road: you cannot describe one without describing the other. Crenshaw's term for the focus on different aspects of oppression – race, class, gender, sexuality, among other factors, which women of colour had been pointing to for many years under other names – has become a key rallying cry and organizing tool for feminist work to follow. Following Crenshaw, sociology professor Patricia Hill Collins further developed and described the ways in which these intersections shape oppression.

In 2000 Jennifer Baumgardner and Amy Richards published *Manifesta*, a book that sat between pop culture and scholarly feminism and explored the links between the 'girl power' of the 90s, characterized by catchy slogans, girl bands and *Buffy the Vampire Slayer*, and the rights-based political battles that remained pressing for young feminists. The authors emphasized that, while celebrating successes, it was still necessary to organize to address ongoing political causes.

In 2001 scholar and activist Emi Koyama coined 'transfeminism', which she described as 'primarily a movement by and for trans women who view their liberation to be intrinsically related to the liberation of all women and beyond. It is also open to other queers, intersex people, trans men, non-trans women, non-trans men, and others who are sympathetic towards the needs of trans women.' Koyama and other transfeminists, including Julia Serano, Patrick Califia and Kate Bornstein, emphasized that biological sex does not determine gender.

The third wave saw the growth and expansion of different branches within feminism. Critiques of the portrayal of women in the media abounded, as well as campaigns against rape culture and sexual harassment. Unlike the second and first waves of feminism, which rallied around the idea that there was at the core of feminism something inextricably linked to the experience of being a woman, the third wave insisted that there was no universal experience of womanhood, and pushed for inclusivity and attention to difference.

THE FOURTH WAVE? (2012–THE PRESENT)

The latter part of the first decade of this century is seen as something of a turning point for both feminist activism and feminist theory. With the internet now seemingly at our collective fingertips, it has become possible to share ideas, information and movements faster than ever before.

In 2011 a 'SlutWalk' was organized in Toronto to tackle

rape culture and the shaming of women, and quickly became an international movement. In the UK, Laura Bates started the website Everyday Sexism in 2014, which caught on nearly instantaneously and has become a significant collection of feminist tools and articles. Also in 2014, when Rebecca Solnit published a collection of essays entitled *Men Explain Things to Me*, the availability of the internet meant that, very quickly, 'mansplaining' found its way into popular usage.

Some of the things that define feminisms today are directly tied to ideas from feminist theory. Women of colour scholars, long arguing for the importance of recognizing multiple oppressions in overlapping identity categories, have provided the grounds for intersectional feminist movements. In 2015 the African American Policy Forum (of which Kimberlé Crenshaw is the director) and the Center for Intersectionality and Social Policy Studies at Columbia Law School launched the #SayHerName campaign in recognition of the black women and girls who have been killed by US police. Intersectionality in feminism is now a key organizing tool. In 2017 the international Women's March, organized by Carmen Perez, Tamika Mallory, Bob Bland and Linda Sarsour as a site of feminist resistance, was also informed by this practice. Queer studies and transfeminisms have become saturated into many of today's feminist movements, with recognition that an inclusive feminism addresses queer and trans communities, too.

*

The presence of the internet has fuelled the fire behind the #MeToo movement, and other movements in which feminists have been involved, including Black Lives Matter campaigns, and the campaign to repeal the Eighth Amendment in the Republic of Ireland. It has helped causes to travel, and has meant that feminist theories can be more accessibly presented.

The internet can also be intimidating! There's a whole world of feminist debate right there on Twitter, and it doesn't always feel like such a welcoming place when you are learning and developing your own opinions. But here's the great news: there are still books! The history of feminist theory outlined above is just one small part of the story, featuring only a few of the players. There's so much more to read and explore, and when you're trying to figure things out, there's nothing like going right to the source. As you set off, don't forget that 'feminism' never means just one thing. There are tangible successes in the history of the movement that we can and should celebrate, there are problems that haven't quite gone away, and tensions, debates and issues that continue to resurface. But, in the midst of this, remember that you can be excited, too! There are so many different ideas for you to chase, so many feminist tasks to take up, and so much space for you to make your own intervention.

"

THERE ARE SO
MANY DIFFERENT
IDEAS FOR YOU
TO CHASE,
SO MANY FEMINIST
TASKS TO TAKE UP,
AND SO MUCH SPACE
FOR YOU TO MAKE
YOUR OWN
INTERVENTION.

"

FURTHER READING

OUR SHARED SHELF

INTRODUCED BY

Emma Watson

ACTOR, ACTIVIST

When I first started Our Shared Shelf, I never dreamed it would become the world's largest feminist book club. I'm so proud of the vibrant global community that has come together and the diverse, respectful opinion-sharing that goes on in this forum.

I often think about how valuable it would have been to have encountered diverse feminist authors and books when I was fourteen or fifteen. What a difference it would have made to the way I viewed myself and interacted with the world. With that in mind, here are ten books selected by Team Our Shared Shelf, specifically for those who are beginning to explore the world and their place in it. With the exception of one, we have not included past book-club selections as we hope you'll seek those out next. At a time when we are too often being reminded of what divides us, there is common ground to be found when we share our stories. Please join me and the conversations at OurSharedShelf.com.

Love,
Emma

THE HATE U GIVE by *Angie Thomas*

This is a book we need. It confronts the police brutality and shooting of unarmed black people in the US that launched the Black Lives Matter movement. But this isn't a novel that looks in from a distance. Angie Thomas tells the story of Starr, a teenage girl thrust into activism as a result of witnessing her friend being killed by the police; someone who constantly has to 'code-switch' to fit in with her suburban, private school friends. She is fighting to find her voice in a world where racialized violence is an everyday reality, and in a movement that could change everything.

BEYOND MAGENTA: TRANSGENDER TEENS SPEAK OUT by *Susan Kuklin*

This collection of accounts from American teens growing up trans is insightful and moving. Each teen tells their story, in their own words, with courage and wisdom. We hope reading this will offer support and guidance to trans teens looking for a voice or story they can identify with on their journey. If you're a cisgendered person who has ever wondered what it is like to grow up trans, these stories will open your eyes. If you're looking to be a better ally, this book composed by author/photographer Susan Kuklin is for you. Given the recent greater awareness and visibility of transgender activists and artists and trans rights, it would be wonderful to see a global update of this revelatory book.

AKATA WITCH by *Nnedi Okorafor*

We're so excited by the Afrofuturism genre! It frames Africa and the diaspora as an integral part of the future of the planet. In the Afrofuture, women and girls lead the way (remember *Black Panther*'s Dora Milaje warriors, and Letitia Wright's role as Shuri, the tech genius princess of Wakanda?). This highly original book by the talented Nnedi Okorafor is about a young American-Nigerian named Sunny. She's an albino, an outsider, and a powerful witch. She's got #blackgirlmagic. And she's a warrior, too.

GIRL UP: KICK ASS, CLAIM YOUR WOMAN CARD AND CRUSH EVERYDAY SEXISM by *Laura Bates*

This is one fierce, laugh-out-loud, no-nonsense guide that tackles head-on what teenage girls are dealing with at a time of savage social media, body-image propaganda and everyday sexism. Laura Bates of the Everyday Sexism project gives us the timely, well-researched book that we wish we'd had as teens.

SOUR HEART by *Jenny Zhang*

Sour Heart is seven tales of seven journeys, all told from the eagle-eyed view of young daughters of new Chinese immigrants to America. These stories reveal the burdensome intimacy shared by families struggling to survive in a strange place, while the young girls fight to carve out their own identities.

So often, we read about what happens to girls, but hardly ever about how they really feel. Poet Jenny Zhang's astounding fiction debut gifts us bold, honest observations that are astute, hilarious, messy and just what we need to hear.

THE UPSIDE OF UNREQUITED
by Becky Albertalli

This is such a funny, sweet book about teenage crushes and LGBTQIA+ love. Molly is into boys, her cool twin, Cassie, is into girls, and their two mums are planning a wedding. Becky Albertalli (author of *Love, Simon*) writes such a relatable narrator. We think a lot of young people will connect with Molly's insecurities about herself, and this fresh, inclusive look at families, love and friendship.

COLONIZE THIS! YOUNG WOMEN OF COLOR
ON TODAY'S FEMINISM edited by Daisy Hernández and
Bushra Rehman

This powerful collection of personal/political essays amplifies the distinct voices of young women of colour in the feminist/womanist movement calling out and confidently pushing back from all corners of the world against the colonialist sins of the patriarchy. Daisy Hernández and Bushra Rehman present us with work that helps shape our consciousness about the cross sections of gender, race, sexuality and class. This book should be required reading for those interested in intersectional feminism.

It's hard to believe *Colonize This!* is now over fifteen years old. We can't wait to read the new edition, which came out in early 2019.

A TIME TO DANCE *by Padma Venkatraman*

This is a tale of a promising young Indian classical dancer who loses her leg in an accident. Adjusting to her prosthetic leg is painful and humbling. Veda has to find a way to reconnect with her spiritual and physical relationship with dance. Padma Venkatraman's story captures the resilience of the human spirit and is beautifully written in verse.

Learning to love our bodies, whatever their form, in societies where we are often judged, body-shamed or sexualized, is a recurring theme that has lessons for us all.

THE THINGS I WOULD TELL YOU
edited by Sabrina Mahfouz

This rich anthology of stories and poems by and about British Muslim women is varied in style and diverse in theme and voice, reflecting the many different backgrounds and experiences of Muslim women.

We so rarely get to read stories like these together. So often, one person of colour's experience or story is expected to represent a whole group. Some of these were written by young women who Sabrina Mahfouz mentored in writing workshops. We need more storytellers like her – willing to amplify moving voices that don't yet have the platform to call out from.

THE BONE SPARROW *by Zana Fraillon*

Can you imagine being born in a refugee camp? Having no frame of reference for anything that exists on the other side of razor wire?

Subhi is a Rohingya boy born to a Burmese refugee mother in a detainment camp in Australia. His boundless imagination and irrepressible spirit are his survival tools.

The shameful headlines about how the world is treating refugees desperately seeking a better life seem endless. We hope Zana Fraillon's poignant tale, based on research and reports from life inside Australian immigration detention centres, helps raise awareness, compassion and alarm bells around the world.

"

AT A TIME WHEN
WE ARE TOO OFTEN
BEING REMINDED OF
WHAT DIVIDES US,
THERE IS COMMON
GROUND TO BE
FOUND WHEN WE
SHARE OUR STORIES.

"

LAST WORDS

WHAT HAPPENS NEXT...

BY

Scarlett Curtis

JOURNALIST, ACTIVIST

There is no perfect feminist. The phrase itself is an oxymoron. Feminists thrive on imperfections. They turn weakness into strength, and vulnerability into power. They take broken systems and find ways to turn the cracks into opportunities, and they take broken girls and find a way to make them feel whole again.

I have spent my whole life, as I think so many women have, feeling like what I had to offer wasn't enough to justify my presence. I have spent years feeling not clever enough, not pretty enough, not cool enough, not fun enough and generally not enough to measure up to what I thought a person should be.

I will not spend my life feeling not feminist enough and neither will you.

You were born, like we all were, with the power inside you to make the world a better place.

Take this book and use it as a weapon. Give it to a friend, give it to an enemy, rip out your favourite page and pin it on your wall.

What you do next is up to you . . . Whether you start a movement or join Girl Up or simply decide to send a nice text to your mum saying thank you, it's all enough, it's all brilliant, it's all something.

Whatever you take from this book, whatever you do next, it's enough.

FEMINISTS CAN WEAR PINK

BY

Scarlett Curtis

JOURNALIST, ACTIVIST

I'm writing this piece exactly one year on from the original publication. If possible, I love feminism even more now than I did when this book was published. If I haven't made that clear enough, let me take this moment to declare it to the world.

I love feminists with a passion that I can only equate to ten-year-old Scarlett's love for Gareth Gates and sticker albums. I have a burning, mind-boggling, life-altering crush on the entire feminist community, but I'm also a little scared of them. I'm scared of them in the way you're scared of a teacher, or a heating bill, or the coolest person in your school. I live in constant fear of taking one wrong step and falling out of favour with this community of superheroes who I am proud to call my friends.

In 2018, when we first put this feminist anthology out into the world, I was terrified. I was a twenty-three-year-old, pink-haired young woman; did I *really* think I was going to be taken seriously as the curator of a book about *anything*, let alone a book about one of the most complex and written about topics in human history?

I had spent five years reading every feminist book I could get my hands on, joining every feminist group I could find and founding my own feminist collective, but it still didn't feel like enough. As the countdown to publication day ticked away, a powerful sense of imposter syndrome wormed its way into my every thought. I was convinced that our book would not be accepted by the only group of people in the world I truly crave respect from. I had nightmares about my favourite feminist activists tweeting that our pink, sparkly essays were 'too frivolous', 'too positive', 'entirely missing the point'.

The third of October 2018 arrived and I was flung into a whirlwind of media and interviews. The idea behind this book was to provide a launchpad for young women to kick off their feminist journey. Our press around its release was focused on reaching teenage girls who might never have read about feminism before.

I THINK OF *FEMINISTS DON'T WEAR PINK & OTHER LIES* AS **A CUTE LITTLE TROJAN HORSE, AN ARTFULLY PACKAGED TOOL OF THE RESISTANCE** DESIGNED TO LURE IN ALL THE WOMEN WHO MIGHT NEVER EVEN HAVE THOUGHT FEMINISM WAS 'FOR THEM'.

We wanted to do something different to tell people that this book existed, to make a statement about how accessible feminism should be. We decided to launch a magical pop-up shop in the mothership of London high-street fashion: Topshop Oxford Circus. On the night of 3 October our amazing (entirely female) team spent the whole night assembling a treasure trove of pink, feminist joy in the basement of the shop.

It's hard to express how excited we all were. As a young girl I spent the majority of my free time meandering through the aisles of this store, searching desperately for a dress or a skirt that might transform me from a teenage girl into the woman I was hoping to become. This shop was where I, like so many girls in this country, grew up. It was where I tried to figure out how to express myself, a place of idols, dreams and visions of adulthood. As our pop-up shop popped up, I squealed with joy at the very idea of a girl in search of a handbag stumbling across a book about feminism and finding herself part of something so exciting, so empowering. The statement 'I used to be a feminist but I changed my mind' has been uttered by exactly zero people throughout history, and I just knew that if we could use this shop to get these ideas into the hands of young women, something powerful was bound to take place.

The fourth of October was a manic day of radio and

podcast interviews, ending with a trip into town to officially launch our pop-up. At lunchtime my editor called me, and then called again, and on her third call I finally picked up the phone. In a confused, frazzled voice she told me that the store had been visited by the senior team first thing that morning. And, after countless hours of work to put it up, our pink, perfect, feminist bubble was dismantled in moments.

Suddenly security was involved, and the team was out of the shop. The culmination of months of work had disappeared, as if it had never existed. This book was published by a team of women in their twenties who could not have worked harder. Our work vanished, and we were literally left out in the cold.

I won't go into greater detail than this. Mostly because I still feel a bit scared of being sued.

It's hard to describe how the few days following this incident felt. When you release a book, the world tends to make you feel like a 'big deal' for a moment. I was on TV, on the radio, my face and words printed in the magazines I had grown up obsessing over. Our book was an outcry of feminist rage and positivity and, after a year of build-up, on the day it was released I felt like we could do anything.

But it took only minutes for my pink, feminist bubble to pop. The reality of what we are dealing with, why we actually need feminism, hit home very, very hard. I crashed down to earth with a body-shaking thud. I arrived at my parents' house in floods of tears, powerlessness seeping through my body. This tiny event felt like a microcosm of everything I had thought we were fighting against. One person can click his fingers and the work and words of women can disappear in moments.

On the day this happened I was told not to say anything about the incident publicly. It was very kind and cautious advice that I swiftly ignored. I tweeted (a lot), and the feminists I had been so terrified to disappoint responded with outcries of resistance.

Topshop responded publicly, too, making a statement about the misunderstanding, and donating £25,000 to our charity partner Girl Up.

This story is a very small one. No one got hurt. In the months following this event, allegations were made about the man who has made so much money from clothing girls; allegations that were not small at all – but also aren't my story to tell. This story is a very small one, but it taught me a very big lesson. The feminist movement has never been bigger or more powerful, but that doesn't mean we don't have enemies. We have real things to fight against, real people and real systems of power that will do everything they can to stop us from succeeding. We are constantly bracing ourselves against laws, individuals and governments who are using their power to hold women back, and we will not succeed in this fight unless we do it together.

When this book came out I was terrified about what 'other feminists' would think of it; in the end, the only objection to our book came from the patriarchy itself. Criticism and comment within the feminist community can be a wonderful thing. From criticism was born intersectionality, trans inclusive feminism, LGBTQ feminism and global feminism. But criticism within our community can also lead to a fear of speaking up.

If you're reading this in the year this paperback is published, it's 2020. Women have never had more rights, more freedom and more autonomy than they do right now – but we also have a seriously long way to go. Less than 20% of the world's landowners are women; 75% of HIV-infected youth between the ages of 15 and 24 are girls; 50% of all sexual assaults worldwide are against girls of 15 or younger; 1 in 7 girls in developing countries is married before the age of 15 (excluding China); in 15 Global Economies a husband is allowed to ban his wife from working; at least 200 million girls and women worldwide have undergone FGM.

These aren't just numbers. They are the basis for gender

inequality, they are the fire that fuels the fearless activism of millions of women across the globe, they are the reason why feminism will not be 'done' until equality is a reality not just for white Western women but for every woman in every corner of the globe. These 'stats' are violations of fundamental human rights that take place every second of every day. These 'stats' are the core of feminism.

We have so much to fight against, we have so many battles still to win. And the main thing I've learned from working with the 52 incredible women in this book, from the charity and publishing teams who helped bring it to life, from the amazing readers who supported us in droves: if we have any hope of achieving anything, we must do it together.

If you're scared to speak up, please know that there will be people who will stand behind you the second you do so. If you're a man who wants to get involved, please know that we have never needed you more, we will let you in. If you're scared to make a mistake, know that you might still have some learning to do, and that's OK. Learn and develop in public. Make friends, make allies, identify the real enemy, and never let anyone trick you into fighting with someone who's already on your side. Join this resistance.

Since this book first came out I have met hundreds of men and women who all believe one thing: that women deserve the right to be equal. Each and every one of them is at a different stage of their feminist journey: some have PhDs and years of activism behind them, some just picked up this book because they liked the cover. All are welcome and all are cherished. Whoever you are, whatever stage you're at, you are in this movement. We need you.

Thank you for being here.

"

MAKE FRIENDS,
MAKE ALLIES,
IDENTIFY THE REAL
ENEMY, AND NEVER
LET ANYONE TRICK YOU
INTO FIGHTING WITH
SOMEONE WHO'S
ALREADY ON YOUR SIDE.
JOIN THIS RESISTANCE.

"

ACKNOWLEDGEMENTS

Thank you to every single contributor in this book for giving us your words and making our world better with your actions. Thank you for inspiring me to be a better person.

Thank you to the incredible, all-female team at Penguin Random House UK and US for believing in a book this mad and for understanding that feminism isn't just a trend.

Thank you to Beth and the team at Girl Up for letting us use this book to help you change the world.

Thank you to May, Eve, Dani, Hen, Bee, Sarah, Martha, Nancy, Lizzie, Crumpet, Ripley, Thandie, Nico, Anna, Millie, Tracey, Jo, Carly, Esther, Posy, Molly, Matilda and Honey for showing me how to be a woman and making me feel more loved than I ever thought I deserved to be.

Thank you to Ol, Dad, Spike, Jake and Char for saving my life over and over again and proving that real men are feminists.

Thank you to my mum for never *telling* me to be a feminist but *showing* me with every choice you make, every word you speak and everything you do.

And finally thank you to Holly for being the best friend a person could have and also a pretty great editor . . .

YOUR THOUGHTS

You can use the following pages to write down your own thoughts on feminism, or to make a note of inspirational quotes – or whatever you want!

FOLLOW @FEMINISTS

Feminists Don't Wear Pink *have launched an Instagram account @feminists, exploring the themes of the book and highlighting some of the amazing members of the Girl Up community. We ask every person featured one very important question:* **What is the one lie you've been told about what it means to be a man or a woman?** *Want to be featured on @feminists? Send a high-res picture of yourself with your answer to this question to:* feminists@penguinrandomhouse.co.uk

TURN
FEELINGS
INTO
THOUGHTS
INTO
ACTIONS.